# The Ultimate Lunchbox Book

Also by the authors

*The 47 Best Chocolate Chip Cookies in the World*
*The Great American Peanut Butter Book*
*The Burger Book*
*The 50 Best Cheesecakes in the World*
*The 50 Best Oatmeal Cookies in the World*
*The 55 Best Brownies in the World*
*Super Sweets*
*The Great International Dessert Cookbook*
*Chocolate Fantasies*

# THE ULTIMATE LUNCHBOX BOOK

*The Best Recipes and Ideas for
Brown Baggers of All Ages from
the Pack-a-Lively Lunchbox Contest*

## Honey and Larry Zisman

*Illustrations by Honey Zisman*

*St. Martin's Griffin* ❧ *New York*

Design by Junie Lee

Library of Congress Cataloging-in-Publication Data

Zisman, Honey.
    The ultimate lunchbox book   :   the best recipes and ideas from the pack-a-lively lunchbox contest   /   Honey and Larry Zisman.
       p.   cm.
    ISBN 0-312-13196-8
    1. Lunchbox cookery.   I. Zisman, Larry.   II. Title.
TX735.Z57   1995                         95-17148
641.5'3—dc20                             CIP

First St. Martin's Griffin Edition: August 1995

10  9  8  7  6  5  4  3  2  1

*For*
*Sean E.*
* * * * * * * *

*May his lunchbox be filled always*
*with*
*marvelous morsels*

# Contents

I opened my lunchbox and what did I see?
A wonderful lunch, made especially for me.
A sandwich, an apple, and of course a sweet;
Everything delightful, all ready to eat.

# The Ultimate Lunchbox Book

# Lunch: It's a Lot More than Just Food at Noon

Lunchtime is much more than just a label on the clock or a time for ingesting sustenance in the middle of the day.

Lunchtime is . . .

- a break from the routine of work and school
- a chance to socialize with friends and colleagues in a congenial atmosphere
- a time to play in the school yard
- the opportunity to impress members of the opposite sex in the school cafeteria
- an opportunity for the hedonistic consumption of extravagant food and drink on an expense account (if you're lucky)
- a free time to think about your plans for tonight, the upcoming weekend, a vacation six months down the road
- a chance to run, jog, ride a bike, play racquetball, and sweat
- an outlet for recreation: to wander, shop, read, play games, and pursue other activities that bring you pleasure
- a time to accomplish all your errands and chores

And, of course, lunchtime is the time for eating the midday meal that will provide you with the energy, nourishment, and vitality to complete whatever activities you are going to do the rest of the day.

If all of us were able to sit down at home in the middle of the day for lunch, we could more easily obtain the advantages and benefits we want to get from lunchtime. But few of us have this luxury, and find it necessary to take our lunches along with us as we leave each morning. Market research done by Tupperware, the company that makes those handy plastic containers, reveals that 30 percent of schoolchildren and 35 percent of working adults take packed food with them when they leave home each day. And, according to the *Tufts University Diet & Nutrition Letter*, in the last 10 years brown bagging of meals and snacks has increased by more than 30 percent.

How we carry our lunches is a matter of personal taste, and the options are vast. We can carry our lunches in Teenage Mutant Ninja Turtles lunchboxes, in expensive leather attaché cases, environmentally correct cotton tote bags, designer pocketbooks, plastic sandwich bags stuffed inside jacket pockets, small insulated ice chests, wildly printed disposable sacks, or just plain old paper bags. It should be noted that a fancy briefcase or a prestige-label handbag is not necessarily more valuable than an illustrated lunchbox. Lunchboxes decorated with cartoon and entertainment characters have become much-sought-after collectibles. For instance, as listed in *The Official Price Guide to Lunch Box Collectibles*, by Scott Bruce, a Wonder Woman lunchbox from 1978 is worth about $50, a 40-year-old Howdy Doody lunchbox can bring about $100, and a 1965 lunchbox with the Beatles on it fetches up to $500.

But no matter what type you choose, it's what's *inside* the lunchbox that counts—and that makes the difference between a ho-hum meal and an enjoyable, rejuvenating experience that you look forward to all morning long—something special that fuels you physically and emotionally for the rest of the day.

*The Ultimate Lunchbox Book* will help ensure that all your away-from-home lunches are exciting and nourishing for both body and soul. The recipes were

---

It may not exactly be the New Jersey Turnpike at rush hour, but it would sure be a crowded roadway.

Think of a highway tunnel 1 mile long, 40 feet wide, and 12 feet high. Now think of it completely filled with sandwiches, salads, soups, fruit, cakes, cookies, drinks, and other assorted foods, and you will have an idea of the estimated volume of all the packed lunches carried to school and work each and every day in the United States.

---

gathered from the nationwide Pack-a-Lively Lunch-box Contest and represent the most delightful, creative, and satisfying lunchtime ideas chosen from thousands of entries. The winners were selected to give you the best possible ways to pack a lunchbox—or whatever else you use to carry your lunch—to make lunchtime extra special for you, your children going each day to school or camp, your spouse away at work, and anyone else whose happiness and well-being at lunchtime depends on what you pack each morning.

Now, read on, choose your favorite foods and ideas, and make lunchtime the ultimate treat, a part of the day that you—or someone important to you—will happily anticipate.

# How to Prepare and Pack the Ultimate Lunchbox

*Hints for Making Lunchbox Preparation a Breeze*

In addition to the prize-winning recipes and lunchtime ideas that you'll find throughout *The Ultimate Lunchbox Book*, we offer a few hints of our own to make packing those meals a whole lot easier.

- Leftovers remaining from dinner can be used to make great lunches. When preparing dinners, think about how the food you are going to serve for dinner can be used for packing lunches. As appropriate, make more than will be eaten at dinnertime to ensure that there will be leftovers. Since most cooked foods can be stored safely in the refrigerator for a day or two, you do not have to pack tonight's leftovers in tomorrow's lunchbox. Try waiting a day before you serve leftovers so that when the lunchbox is opened there won't be the cry, "I just had it for dinner last night."

- To prevent sandwich bread from becoming soggy, make sure that lettuce leaves and sliced vegetables are thoroughly dry before putting them into the sandwich. Another suggestion for keeping bread fresh until lunchtime is to coat both slices of bread, not just the top or the bottom slice, with some type of spread such as margarine, peanut butter, mayonnaise, or mustard.

- Sandwiches do not have to be made just on white, rye, or whole wheat bread—or even on bread at all. Think of bagels, hot dog rolls, pitas, muffins, English muffins, matzoh, croissants, tortillas, taco shells, biscuits, rice cakes, scones, and all kinds of crackers. Graham crackers are especially good for making peanut butter and jelly sandwiches and cream cheese and jelly sandwiches.

- While nutrition, of course, is an important consideration when packing lunches, do not be overconcerned if occasionally the meals you pack are not absolutely nutritionally perfect. The important thing to remember is that it is undesirable eating habits, rather than an undesirable food every so often, that can be harmful. Do not become obsessed with making every packed lunch nutritionally balanced and correct.
- When eating at fast-food and self-service restaurants, save those extra unopened little packets of ketchup, mustard, and mayonnaise. Include them with the lunches you pack in case someone wants an additional amount of the condiments you put on the sandwiches.
- Some of the foods you put into a lunchbox can be easily squashed, so use rigid plastic containers with lids to protect delicate items.
- Many packaged foods can be kept without refrigeration and packed with lunches without fear of spoiling. Even some packaged foods that are kept refrigerated in the store and at home can be put into a lunchbox and safely eaten three or four hours later. Ask at the store where you buy the food how long it can be left out of the refrigerator before eating.
- Thermos bottles are not just for coffee and

---

"Ugh!" Not in My Lunchbox

To ensure that the lunches you make are eaten, rather than discarded because your children do not like what has been packed, maintain an "Ugh! List" on which they can put—and take off—those foods that they don't like or don't want to be seen eating. This list can be on a write-on/wipe-off board kept right in the kitchen for easy reference and easy additions and subtractions.

Scott Reeder
Arlington, Texas

---

cold drinks. The widemouth varieties can be useful for packing all kinds of soups and one-dish meals, keeping them hot and delicious until it is time to eat. The old trick of rinsing a Thermos bottle with hot tap water or ice water before putting hot or cold foods in it is still a good idea. An alternative is to let the Thermos sit uncovered overnight in the freezer before filling with cold food.
- Containers of frozen juice and sandwiches

made with frozen bread can be packed in a lunchbox while still frozen. They will thaw out within a couple of hours and be ready to enjoy at lunchtime. (Since some home freezers can be extremely cold, it is a good idea to test beforehand the defrosting rate of the frozen juice to make sure that it will, indeed, defrost by lunchtime.) The frozen foods are also useful in keeping other foods cold should that be necessary.

- Since lunchboxes and lunch bags might be stored in a variety of different places—a refrigerator, a high school locker, a desk drawer—consider the storage conditions when packing food. And remember that just because it is winter does not mean that the lunch will be stored in a cold place. In fact, there is a good chance that storage areas in wintertime might be hotter than during spring and fall. The increased heat during cold weather results from the heating systems in operation. Heating ducts and pipes pass through closets and other small, closed areas, making them much warmer than usual.

- Although you may have definite ideas on providing only "good" foods for lunch and leaving out all "bad" foods, your selection process will mean nothing if your children do not eat what you pack. It is extremely important to consult your

---

## ALWAYS BETTER SAFE THAN SORRY

Considering all the possible food contaminants in the news, keep in mind how the lunches you pack will be stored until they are eaten at noontime or later. This is especially important during hot weather, when food can spoil more readily. Of course, you could use frozen gel packs or frozen juice containers. Frozen juice serves a double purpose: It keeps the food cold *and* provides a beverage for lunch.

Elizabeth Dean
Little Rock, Arkansas

---

children on their likes, dislikes, and changing feelings about what they want for lunch. Someone who has eaten ham and cheese for lunch every day for six months may all of a sudden develop an intense dislike for ham and cheese and then want only peanut butter and banana sandwiches. Keeping yourself well informed is important so you can know that packed foods become eaten foods.

- In addition to getting your children's input

about the foods they like and dislike, it can also be worthwhile and rewarding to have them participate in making their lunches. They will not only learn the mechanics of packing lunches but also get a sense of involvement in a grown-up activity and self-satisfaction that they are working to take care of their own needs.

- It is always risky to surprise someone with new and different foods in his or her lunchbox. Besides the shock of not getting what is expected, there is also a good chance that the new food will not be liked. This can be very discouraging, especially if no alternative meal is readily available at lunchtime. Always try out new foods at home during a meal or as a snack to ensure that unpleasant surprises do not ruin someone's day.

- While having a ham sandwich or sliced zucchini twice in one day is not a major disaster, consider what has been served at breakfast and what will be served at dinner and then pack the lunch accordingly to give variety to the three meals of the day.

- When asking people what they want for lunch, it is usually better to give a choice of several items rather than to pose the completely open-ended question, "What do you want me to make for your lunch?" You can limit the choices to what is on hand in the house, what can be readily obtained, and what foods you prefer making, so that you do not create for yourself a burdensome chore.

- It can be easily overlooked, but a lunchbox should be washed just as often as any dish or piece of silverware: after every use. In addition, rinse out the lunchbox with baking soda several times a month to dispose of any odors.

- Since some foods require utensils for eating, keep a supply of inexpensive, disposable plastic forks and spoons on hand to include with a packed lunch for school. Do not include real silverware; the chances are too great that it will get lost between home and school.

## Answers to the Most Frequently Asked Questions about Lunchbox Preparation and Packing

**Question:** My daughter is in 6th grade, and for the last year and a half the only thing she will take to school for lunch is a tuna salad sandwich. I have offered to make her anything she wants—from peanut butter and jelly to corned beef sandwiches, from cold pizza to pasta salad—but the only thing she wants is tuna. What can I do to get her to eat a variety of foods for lunch?

**Answer:** Quick and not unreasonable answers to your question are two more questions: "What's the problem?" and "Why bother?" Tuna fish is a nutritious food, and as long as you don't overload the mayonnaise when making the sandwich, you are not giving her too much fat. Just add some lettuce and tomato (wrap them separately from the sandwich for adding at lunchtime so she doesn't get a soggy sandwich) and use whole wheat bread. Not to worry—your daughter is eating a good lunch.

Not to be overlooked is the fact that your daughter's lunchtime preference makes life pretty easy for you. You don't have the daily aggravation of finding out what your child wants and then making sure you have it in the house. There are no decisions to be made, and all you have to do is keep a supply of tuna fish cans in the pantry—and refrain from serving tuna casserole for dinner.

**Question:** Every day I prepare a really nice lunch—tasty, nutritionally correct, attractively packed—for my son, who's in 1st grade, and every day he trades most of it for different food from his friends. Why doesn't he eat what I make for him?

**Answer:** The person who should be asked about his lunch is your son—he may give you the real answer. The main questions to ask are, "What is he trading away?" and "What is he getting in return?" The answers to those questions should give you a good idea of your child's likes and dislikes.

If he is trading away the "good" nutritious sandwiches for "bad" nonnutritious cakes and cookies, there may be a larger problem than just the lunchtime eating situation. Some nutritional education may be needed, and the good food may need to be presented in a form that will be eaten rather than traded away.

It is important to recognize children's likes and dislikes—even if they are not our own or not 100 percent nutritionally sound—and to prepare the right food for them in such a way that it will have the best chance of being eaten. You cannot go to school and stand over him at lunch and force him to eat what you want him to eat. All you can do is prepare his lunch so it is appetizing and appealing to him; then he will be more likely to eat it rather than trade it for something else.

**Question:** My 3rd grader frequently forgets to bring his lunchbox home with him from school at the end of the day and sometimes even leaves leftover food in it. What can I do to get him to remember to bring it home?

**Answer:** The immediate solution is to pack his lunch in a paper bag. As for a long-term solution, you might consider talking to his teacher to see if he could give a gentle lunchbox reminder to your son when school is over. Perhaps you could put a note in your son's shirt or coat pocket with the word LUNCHBOX in big red letters.

Although bribing children to do what they should do on their own is not always a good idea, here is a suggestion that might be useful. Cut up a fake dollar bill into about 10 pieces. Place one piece of the bill in the lunchbox each day, and after he brings home all 10 pieces, he gets a whole dollar in exchange. The sooner he brings home all 10 pieces, the sooner he gets his dollar.

Just remember that children are always forgetting things—from the house key to their glasses—and be sure you have plenty of paper bags available.

**Question:** What can I do about the changing styles in lunchboxes? You know how important it is for kids to carry the right type of lunchbox. Unfortunately, each year—or even sooner—what's "in" and what's "out" changes. The old lunchbox is then unacceptable, and it becomes social suicide to be seen carrying it to school.

**Answer:** Frankly, there's probably nothing you can do about the fickleness in lunchbox fashions except to buy a new lunchbox—or have your child ostracized by his peers. (Think about how the style of men's ties changes from year to year—or the length of women's skirts.)

Just view the cost of a new lunchbox every so often as part of the price you have to pay for living in a fashion-oriented society.

*Question:* This is not really a question but a suggestion you might want to pass on. My daughter is always losing her pencil in school, so I make sure that there is always a pencil in her lunchbox for a replacement at the start of the afternoon.

*Answer:* Thanks for your suggestion. It sounds like a good idea. There are probably other items that could be put into a lunchbox on a regular basis as a replacement storage case for frequently misplaced items. Those items—whether a house key, extra money, or even an extra pair of socks on a rainy day—can give a feeling of security to someone who is sometimes forgetful.

*Question:* My children really like to eat peeled and cut-up apples, but how do you avoid having them turn brown if they are not eaten right away?

*Answer:* Besides the traditional technique of coating the apple slices with lemon juice and wrapping them tightly in plastic wrap or aluminum foil, there are some fun ways to keep them looking fresh. Spread cream cheese, peanut butter, marshmallow creme, or apple butter over each piece, or press a piece of cheese tightly against the apple slices. Of course, the apple will still have to be well wrapped, but you will have that added protection—and added nutrition—of the food covering.

*Question:* I have made and packed more lunches than I ever want to count all through the years my children were in elementary and then junior high school. Now that they are in high school, isn't it time that they did it for themselves?

*Answer:* Amen to that! There is no reason for parents to continue doing things for their children that the children can do for themselves. And packing lunches is one of them. There may be a problem in making sure that a good lunch is packed each day, so keep appropriate foods available in the house and provide some low-key guidance on what is included.

*Question:* What can I do when my children say that on some days the lunch sold in the school cafeteria is better than the lunch they brought with them and they wished they could have the school lunch instead?

*Answer:* While not encouraging any wasting of food, it might be a worthwhile idea to have a special pocket or envelope in each child's lunchbox labeled IN THE

EVENT OF LUNCHTIME EMERGENCY, OPEN ENVELOPE. Inside the envelope could be enough money to buy a school lunch on those days when that choice is more attractive.

There should be a limit to how often a "lunchtime emergency" can occur each week or month. It would also be a good idea to encourage giving the uneaten packed lunch to friends, to minimize any waste of food.

*Question:* Next year my son will be starting school and eating lunch in the cafeteria there. I am concerned about how he will adjust to eating lunch away from home. Is there any way to make that adjustment easier?

*Answer:* One way to make it easier to adapt to eating lunch at school rather than at home would be to have a dress rehearsal. Try this: Go with him to the store and pick out a lunchbox. While he is still at home for the whole day, make and pack a complete lunch for him in his lunchbox. You could pack your own lunch in a paper bag, as part of the fun. Let him know that at lunchtime he can open his lunchbox, just like the big kids do at school. Encourage him to look forward to the noon hour, and then join him for a great lunch.

*Question:* Considering how many lunches are carried to school and to work each day, I am convinced there is some type of business connected with making and packing lunches that I could start and do from home. Do you have any ideas?

*Answer:* The preparation and sale of food products from the home is subject to a great many health, zoning, and other regulations, and, in fact, in some places such activities are absolutely illegal. And, then, of course, there is the exorbitant cost of liability insurance to protect you in case someone claims he or she got sick from your food.

There is, however, a good lunch-oriented business you can start, which doesn't involve any food. Why not get plain lunchboxes and decorate them with paintings or other artwork and sell them at local craft fairs? Your designer lunchboxes could become a big hit, local boutiques and gourmet shops might stock them, and you could become a local celebrity. (You might also do this for your own children. See the next question.)

*Question:* My daughter in junior high school is tired of carrying the same kind of lunchbox that everyone else has, which looks as if it were bought at a discount store (she is one of the few who doesn't want to do what everyone else is doing). Do you have any suggestions to accommodate her newfound individuality and fashion consciousness?

*Answer:* Why not help her decorate her lunchbox with pictures and designs that have a connection to her personal interests and hobbies, such as sports, music, movies, animals, and science? It is quite possible that her friends will really like what they see your daughter carrying to school and want something special for themselves. Then you will have the seeds of a potential new business. (See the preceding question.)

If you do start making and selling decorated lunchboxes, just be sure that your daughter's lunchbox retains its uniqueness.

*Question:* My son refuses to carry a lunchbox and will use only a plain paper bag. On rainy days his lunch bag is usually soaked by the time he gets to school. What can I do to make sure that his lunch bag stays dry?

*Answer:* Those clear plastic sandwich bags do not just have to go inside the paper bag. On rainy days put the entire lunch bag inside a large plastic bag, and it will stay dry on the trip to school. As you can see by the next question, sandwich bags have other uses.

*Question:* A frequent complaint by my son is that the refrigerator at school, where his lunch stays all morning, is smelly and his lunch picks up odors. How can I shield his lunch from those odors?

*Answer:* Put your son's lunch bag inside a large plastic sandwich bag. Such bags are convenient and will protect his food from absorbing any odors.

*Question:* How do I cope with the pieces of bread I always find leftover in my son's lunchbox when he comes home from school? More often than not he eats the insides of a sandwich and leaves the bread.

*Answer:* You describe a very common situation, for which there are easy solutions. If your son does not like a particular kind of bread, just find out what kind he likes and use that for making sandwiches.

Or perhaps he has just gotten tired of sandwiches but likes the fillings. Try packing the tuna salad, meat, cheese, or whatever you usually give him in the sandwich, in a separate container. Include a plastic spoon or fork and let him eat the food as an entrée instead of as a sandwich. You can pack different types of rolls, muffins, biscuits, or breads as part of a nonsandwich lunch.

*Question:* My daughter received a family heirloom doll from her grandmother. It is a small doll, and now she wants to take it with her everywhere, especially in her lunchbox to preschool so that it can keep her company while she eats. That doll, however, is rather valuable, both financially and sentimentally, and I'm afraid it will be lost or damaged. How do I get her to leave it home without simply forbidding her to take it to preschool?

*Answer:* Why don't you get another small doll that could be the "lunchbox friend" of the heirloom doll? Send the "friend" to preschool in the lunchbox each day. When preschool is over, the new doll can report back to her "heirloom friend," telling everything that went on in preschool.

---

Lunchboxes have evolved a great deal since the days when children used old tobacco tins to carry their lunches to school each day.

The first licensed lunchbox with a character on it was the Mickey Mouse lunchbox that appeard in 1935. But it was not until 1950 that the lunchbox character craze really took off with the introduction of a lunchbox that featured pictures of Hopalong Cassidy, the television cowboy hero. More than a half million copies of that lunchbox were sold.

The best-selling lunchbox of all time was the Disney School Bus, which sold more than two million copies between 1961 and 1973.

The Hopalong Cassidy lunchbox may be no more than a ghost from the past—albeit a valuable collectible ghost—but it has been replaced by an almost endless choice, including:

- insulated waterproof nylon bags with a touch-and-close seal and top and decorated with National Football League team logos and colors on the sides
- black-and-white pony-print cotton mini-briefcases with a zipper top
- softsided, insulated lunch kits decorated with pictures of a choice of numerous characters, in-

cluding Superman, Batman, X-Men, Spider-Man, Barney, and Marsupilami
- lunchboxes that look like rocks, just like the lunchboxes carried by the guys in the *Flintstones* movie
- lunch "shells" that are shaped like seashells and even have a small shell compartment on the front panel for storage of small items
- insulated "lunch purses" for girls, complete with a shoulder strap, a pocket for personal belongings, an unbreakable mirror, and pictures of Barbie, The Little Mermaid, Lamb Chop, or Thumbelina

Perhaps the most elaborate lunchbox of all—but not really the choice for a 3rd grader to take to school each day—is the 3-pound Stove-To-Go combination lunchbox and oven that can be plugged into the cigarette lighter of a car or truck or into a standard electrical outlet. The heating element in the bottom goes up to a temperature of 300°F and can be used to warm entire meals, canned foods, and leftovers.

It is altogether appropriate that there is such an extensive variety of lunchboxes available on the market, since about seven million of them are sold each year.

# 3

# ULTIMATE RENDITIONS OF THE TOP FIVE LUNCHBOX CLASSICS

**W**hat is more traditional and classic than these popular sandwiches?

Peanut Butter and Jelly
Tuna Salad
Egg Salad
Chicken Salad
Ham and Cheese

And what would be more appropriate than making the ultimate sandwiches from this celebrated group of lunchtime favorites?

So in addition to having all the prize-winning recipes in the Pack-a-Lively Lunchbox Contest included in *The Ultimate Lunchbox Book*, we have created our own special versions of these sandwiches:

The Ultimate Peanut Butter and Jelly Sandwich
The Ultimate Tuna Salad Sandwich
The Ultimate Egg Salad Sandwich
The Ultimate Chicken Salad Sandwich
The Ultimate Ham (Etc.) and Cheese Sandwich Collection

# The Ultimate Peanut Butter and Jelly Sandwich

3 tablespoons chunky peanut butter
3 slices white bread
1½ tablespoons orange marmalade

1½ tablespoons marshmallow creme
½ cup shredded cheddar cheese

Spread 1 tablespoon peanut butter on one slice of bread. Spread marmalade over top. Set aside.

Spread 1 tablespoon peanut butter on another slice of bread and then place on top of marmalade, peanut butter side down. Spread marshmallow creme on exposed side of bread. Sprinkle cheese over top of marshmallow creme. Set aside.

Spread remaining peanut butter on remaining slice of bread and then place on top of cheese, forming a double-decker sandwich.

*Yield: 1 sandwich*

Is there a more popular sandwich among school-children than that old standard of peanut butter and jelly?

Absolutely not!

And, not surprisingly, grape jelly is the most popular of all store-bought jellies. But grape's popularity is no reason to avoid trying some other interesting and tasty varieties of jellies, jams, preserves, marmalades, and all-fruit spreads. The variety is great and growing each day as new and exotic flavors are added.

What about peanut butter?

More than seven hundred million pounds of peanut butter are eaten every year in the United States. Figuring two tablespoons of peanut butter in each sandwich, that is enough peanut butter to make ten billion "PB & J" sandwiches.

And a goodly number of those sandwiches are carried to school every day. More than 80 percent of grade-school children who bring their lunch to school carry peanut butter and jelly sandwiches.

# THE ULTIMATE TUNA SALAD SANDWICH

1 6⅛-ounce can tuna, drained
2 tablespoons chopped black olives
2 tablespoons chopped walnuts
½ cup chopped peeled apple
2 tablespoons mayonnaise

1 teaspoon fresh lemon juice
salt
pepper
2 slices whole wheat bread

Combine tuna, olives, walnuts, apple, mayonnaise, lemon juice, salt, and pepper. Spoon onto one slice of bread and top with the other.
*Yield: 1 sandwich*

Good-quality wax paper actually has a triple coating of highly refined, odorless, tasteless, and oil-free wax.

Wax is forced into the pores of the paper itself and then spread over each side of the paper as a coating. This triple coating helps to make the paper transparent so you can see whatever is wrapped inside.

# THE ULTIMATE EGG SALAD SANDWICH

3 hard-boiled eggs, mashed
1 teaspoon apricot jam
$\frac{1}{2}$ teaspoon Dijon mustard
1 tablespoon mayonnaise
1 sweet gherkin pickle, chopped

4 dried apricots, chopped
salt
pepper
4 lettuce leaves
2 soft rolls, sliced

Combine eggs, apricot jam, mustard, mayonnaise, pickle, apricots, salt, and pepper.

Divide into 2 portions and spread onto the bottoms of the rolls. Cover each filling with 2 lettuce leaves and the top of the roll.

*Yield: 2 sandwiches*

---

Three things you might have wanted to know about aluminum foil:

1. Aluminum foil has been around as a common household product for more than 50 years.
2. Aluminum foil is about 98.5 percent aluminum, with iron and silicon added to give it strength and make it resistant to puncture.
3. It doesn't matter which side—shiny or dull—is wrapped against the food. The shine on one side comes from the manufacturing process as the aluminum foil is rolled into thin sheets.

# THE ULTIMATE CHICKEN SALAD SANDWICH

¾ cup diced cooked chicken
¼ cup finely chopped cabbage
¼ cup dried cranberries
½ cup halved seedless red grapes
2 teaspoons mayonnaise

1 teaspoon sour cream
salt
pepper
2 pita pockets

Combine chicken, cabbage, cranberries, grapes, mayonnaise, sour cream, salt, and pepper. Divide into 2 portions and spoon into pita pockets.
*Yield: 2 sandwiches*

Have you ever wondered how Wonder bread got its name—or about the design on the wrapper?

In 1921, the Taggert Baking Company of Indianapolis was planning to introduce a new loaf of bread. Elmer Cline, the vice president of the bakery, was put in charge of creating a name for the new bread.

While contemplating his important task, Mr. Cline happened to go to the International Balloon Race, which was being held at the Indianapolis Speedway. At this event, he was inspired by the hundreds of colorful balloons up in the sky. The sight of all those balloons was full of wonder to him, and he knew that he had found a name for the new bread.

But Mr. Cline did not stop with just the name. Check the Wonder bread wrapper and you will see the colorful balloons that have decorated its packages since this product was first put on the market.

In 1930, Wonder bread was made available in sliced loaves, a major innovation at that time. The packages of individually sliced bread were first received with considerable suspicion, but then consumers enthusiastically embraced the convenience of not having to cut the loaves of bread themselves.

Today, Wonder is the best-selling brand of bread in the United States.

# The Ultimate Ham (Etc.) and Cheese Sandwich Collection

Prosciutto and Provolone
Corned Beef and Finlandia Swiss
Smoked Turkey and Brie
Pastrami and Edam
Sopressata and Boursin
Roast Pork and Muenster
Salami and Bianco
Bacon and Roquefort
Roast Beef and Camembert
Virginia Ham and Cheddar
Liverwurst and Liederkranz
Copacola and Havarti
Pepper Ham and Jarlsberg
Cajun Roast Beef and Gruyère
Lebanon Bologna and Sweet Munchie

It is entirely appropriate that the makers of Grey Poupon mustard make a big deal that their mustard is made with white wine, since the word "mustard" comes from the Latin *mustum*, the "must" or grape juice that is used to make wine.

But mustard is much more than just wine. It is the second most widely used spice in the United States after black pepper.

It should be no surprise that French's yellow mustard is the best-selling mustard in the world. The next most popular type is, of course, the brown variety—with a little more bite—exemplified by Gulden's spicy brown mustard.

Yellow and brown mustards, however, are just the tip of the proverbial iceberg when it comes to the wide array of mustards available. Just visit the mustard section of any supermarket or, even better, any gourmet food shop, and you will be able to contemplate more types and mixtures than you ever thought possible—or, perhaps, necessary.

Be adventurous with mustard and make your lunchtime sandwiches a new experience.

# 4

# Soups

*At school or work, there is nothing more satisfying than homemade soup for comfort and enjoyment.*

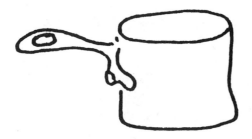

# BETTER CHEDDAR SOUP
## *Lisa Reed*
### BLOOMINGTON, INDIANA

2 tablespoons margarine or butter
2 tablespoons flour
2 cups milk or cream
½ teaspoon salt

½ teaspoon mustard
1 beef bouillon cube dissolved in ½ cup boiling water
3 cups grated cheddar cheese

Place margarine in a heavy saucepan and melt over low heat. Stir in flour and cook for 1 minute. Stir in milk and continue cooking until thick and smooth. Add salt, mustard, and dissolved bouillon cube. Stir until thoroughly mixed. Add cheese and continue cooking and stirring until cheese has melted.

*Yield: 2 to 4 servings*

---

### ROAMING WHILE YOU'RE EATING

If you, like many people, need to be reached by telephone even during the lunch hour, you are stuck at your desk. But having a cellular telephone lets you go out to a park, walk along the waterfront, or do many other activities during lunchtime, still reachable but not confined to the office.

Robin Abrams
Oak Lawn, Illinois

---

# GAZPACHO IN A FLASH
## *Kristen Fleming*
### MADISON, NEW JERSEY

1 large garlic clove, peeled
1 small onion, peeled and cut into quarters
2 cucumbers, peeled and cut into quarters
3 large ripe tomatoes, cut into quarters and peeled
3 tablespoons olive oil

2 tablespoons wine vinegar
½ teaspoon basil
dash pepper
1 46-ounce can tomato juice
Italian bread

Place garlic, onion, cucumbers, tomatoes, olive oil, wine vinegar, basil, pepper, and tomato juice in a food processor and process until thoroughly blended.

Chill in refrigerator.

Serve cold with chunks of Italian bread.

*Yield: 6 servings*

---

## CLEANUP MADE EASIER

It is easy to overlook, but cleanup is part of the lunchtime routine. Make it less of a chore by including several individual packets of wash-up napkins. If you have run out of them when packing your lunch, you can always use instead some wet paper towels in a sealed plastic sandwich bag.

Nora Anderson
Lakewood, Colorado

# FRANKLY GOOD PEA SOUP
*Emily Lund*
BROOKLYN CENTER, MINNESOTA

*4 hot dogs, cut into thin slices*
*1 8½-ounce can peas, puréed*
*1 cup beef broth*

*2 tablespoons cream or milk*
*dash garlic powder*

Fry hot dog slices and then place in a heavy saucepan along with the puréed peas, beef broth, cream, and garlic powder.

Cook over low heat for approximately 20 minutes.

*Yield: 2 servings*

The plain, ubiquitous Thermos bottle filled with coffee that was found in every workman's lunch pail has blossomed to new status as a utilitarian fashion statement and has even become a desired and cherished wedding present.

Initially manufactured almost 90 years ago, Thermos bottles were first used just for keeping coffee hot. Now, carried to school and work, they come with regular-size tops for beverages; with wide-mouth tops for hot soups and stews and for cold fruit salads and pasta salads; and with convenient Twist 'N' Pour stoppers. Coffee-cone tops are also available for brewing fresh coffee right into a Thermos bottle.

Boaters and fishermen are not left out. For them, there is a floating Thermos bottle that will not sink even when full.

And they make great gifts.

In Central and South America, Thermos bottles are popular and very practical gifts given at weddings and baby showers. Parents use them to keep hot water in the baby's room for late night feedings. Having the hot water readily available for making formula is a great convenience.

# Quick and Easy Tomato-Crab Bisque

*Carol Bowman*

Evanston, Illinois

*1 6-ounce can crab meat, drained*
*1 10½-ounce can tomato soup*
*10½ ounces milk*

*2 tablespoons sherry*
*hot pepper sauce to taste*
*Worcestershire sauce to taste*

Mix together crab meat, tomato soup, milk, and sherry and heat to boiling in a heavy saucepan. Reduce heat and let simmer for 3 to 4 minutes.

Add hot pepper sauce and Worcestershire as desired.

*Yield: 2 servings*

It keeps food fresh, it can be used over and over again for years and years, it can be filled with food and taken in a lunchbox without any fears of leaking, and its designs have earned it places in the collections of the Brooklyn Museum of Art, the Cooper-Hewitt Museum, the Museum of Modern Art, and the Metropolitan Museum of Art (all in New York City); the National History Museum of the Smithsonian Institution in Washington, D.C.; and the Victoria and Albert Museum in London.

In Japan such items are called Kimona Keepers and Bento Boxes; in Korea, Kimchee Keepers; and in South America, Tortilla Keepers.

We are talking about—what else?—Tupperware.

These handy containers are the invention of Earl Tupper, a self-educated chemist and industrial designer in New Hampshire. In the 1940s he started by turning a black, hard-as-rock, foul-smelling chunk of polyethylene slag (a waste product of oil refining) into the plastic food-storage boxes that are now sold in 56 countries.

More than eighty million people each year attend Tupperware parties; one starts somewhere around the world every three seconds.

The popularity of Tupperware in this country can be readily seen. If you have a Tupperware product in your home, yours is among the more than 90 percent of all American households that have at least one piece of Tupperware.

# 5

## SANDWICHES

*There's more to life than just two slices of white bread with peanut butter and jelly.*

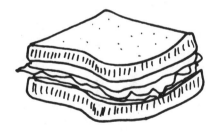

# THE SOPHISTICATED CHEESE SANDWICH
## *Sara Scanlon*
### QUINCY, MASSACHUSETTS

6 ounces cream cheese, softened
2 ounces blue cheese, softened
2 tablespoons parsley
$\frac{1}{4}$ teaspoon paprika
$\frac{1}{3}$ cup finely chopped walnuts

1 tablespoon grated onion
$\frac{1}{2}$ teaspoon Worcestershire sauce
$\frac{1}{2}$ cup finely crushed bran flakes
lettuce
6 slices rye or pumpernickel bread

Combine cream cheese, blue cheese, parsley, paprika, walnuts, onion, and Worcestershire sauce, mixing together well. Mix in bran flakes.

Place cheese mixture along with lettuce on bread.

*Yield: 3 sandwiches*

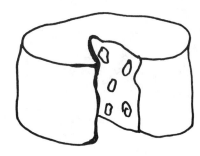

Why do we pay daily homage to a corrupt, incompetent, scandalous, and all-around disreputable English nobleman who was, during his lifetime, the British secretary of state, the postmaster general, the First Lord of the Admiralty, and . . . a notorious compulsive gambler?

We honor him because he was John Montagu, the fourth Earl of Sandwich, who lived in 18th-century England and inadvertently gave us what is probably our most commonly eaten culinary creation.

During a 24-hour marathon gambling session in 1762, the Earl of Sandwich was reluctant to leave the gaming tables and ordered his servant to bring him meat and bread arranged in such a way that he could eat them while continuing to gamble.

To satisfy the Earl, the servant placed the meat between two slices of bread, and thus was born the sandwich. Of course, it was named after this unsavory character who, with his mind totally consumed by the action on the table, never realized his name was going to be immortalized for his quick snack.

It is not recorded whether the Earl left the gaming tables a winner or loser that day, but regardless of the financial results, he earned for himself an important place in world history.

# Eggstraordinary Salad Sandwich
### Nell Fowler
#### Lawrence, Kansas

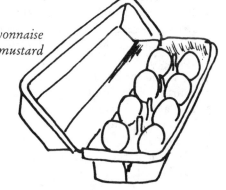

4 hard-boiled eggs, finely chopped
¼ cup raisins
¼ cup finely chopped grapes
¼ cup finely chopped pecans

3 tablespoons mayonnaise
1 teaspoon Dijon mustard
4 slices rye bread

Mix together eggs, raisins, grapes, pecans, mayonnaise, and mustard.
Spread on rye bread.
*Yield: 2 sandwiches*

---

For sandwich spreads, there are butter, margarine, mayonnaise, mustard, ketchup, Russian dressing, and, of course, Benedictine sandwich spread.

What—you never heard of Benedictine sandwich spread?

Just take some softened cream cheese, thin it with mayonnaise, add chopped-up onion and cucumber, and then mix in some chopped spinach or parsley until you get a nice green color. (Or you can skip the green vegetables and just use green food coloring.)

It is believed that Benedictine sandwich spread was invented by a caterer in Louisville, Kentucky, who evidently liked bright green food.

# PEANUT BUTTER AND TURKEY THING

*Arnold Simmons*

JACKSONVILLE, ARKANSAS

½ cup chunky peanut butter
2 slices whole grain bread
2 tablespoons orange marmalade

¼ cup chopped celery
turkey slices
lettuce

Spread peanut butter on both slices of bread. Spread orange marmalade over the peanut butter on one slice of bread and sprinkle the celery over the peanut butter on the other slice. Layer the turkey slices and lettuce over the marmalade and cover with the celery and peanut butter bread.

*Yield: 1 sandwich*

---

### VARIETY IS THE SPICE OF LUNCH

An amazing assortment of breads and rolls is now available for making sandwiches. Look around your supermarket, specialty food stores, and fresh bakeries for something new to use instead of old-fashioned white bread. You can probably use a different type of bread for sandwiches for an entire month without having the same bread twice.

Priscilla Smith
Springdale, South Carolina

# CRABMEAT SANDWICH
*Tanya Wheeler*
WESTERVILLE, OHIO

1 4-ounce can crabmeat, drained
8 ounces cream cheese, softened
3 tablespoons chopped onion
2 tablespoons chopped chives

1 tablespoon lemon juice
$\frac{1}{4}$ teaspoon paprika
2 soft rolls

Combine crabmeat, cream cheese, onion, chives, lemon juice, and paprika.
Spoon into rolls.
*Yield: 2 sandwiches*

---

### THE PROFESSIONAL LUNCHBOX

If you take your lunch to work in a briefcase or an attaché case, pack it inside one of those expandable wallet files with a closable flap rather than just in a paper bag. You won't experience the embarrassment of opening your attaché case at a morning meeting and having your lunch be the most noticeable thing in your briefcase or, worse yet, having an apple from your lunch bag fall out and roll across the conference table. It's a small step you can take to protect your professional image.

Harold Kroll
Washington, D.C.

# HAPPY HOAGIE
## *Carl Yang*
### ANN ARBOR, MICHIGAN

1 12- to 14-inch loaf Italian bread
mayonnaise
olive oil
vinegar
dried oregano
1 onion, sliced
1 large tomato, sliced

2 large pimientos, sliced
4 slices provolone cheese
4 slices copacola
4 slices prosciutto
shredded lettuce
hot peppers, optional to taste

Slice Italian bread lengthwise. Spread one side with mayonnaise and sprinkle oil and vinegar on the other side. Sprinkle oregano over both sides.

Place onion, tomato, pimientos, provolone cheese, copacola, prosciutto, and lettuce in sandwich. Add hot peppers if desired.

Cut in half.

*Yield: 2 sandwiches*

## Absolutely, Positively, Lunch "To Go"

Schoolchildren frequently go on trips during the school day, so lunches for those days should receive special consideration. Will the lunch sit in a hot bus rather than stay in a cool classroom or in a refrigerator until noon? Is the usual lunch that is prepared a little too messy or complicated to eat while riding along? Will children be too excited about the trip to eat everything you usually include in the lunch? Think of the special circumstances of each trip and plan the lunch accordingly.

Elaine Howell
Salem, Oregon

# CHEDDAR APPLE SANDWICH
## Teresa Cooper
### GREENSBORO, NORTH CAROLINA

2 tablespoons plain yogurt
1 tablespoon wheat germ
1 teaspoon spicy brown mustard
2 slices whole wheat bread

1 large apple, cored, peeled, sliced, and brushed with
    orange juice
¼ cup shredded cheddar cheese

Combine yogurt, wheat germ, and mustard and spread on bread slices. Layer apple slices and sprinkle cheese over top.
*Yield: 1 sandwich*

---

**The challenge:** to eat the most sandwiches in the shortest amount of time
**The reason:** to get into the *Guinness Book of World Records*
**The winner:** Peter Dowdeswell
**The place:** The Donut Shop in Reedley, California

**The number of sandwiches:** 40
**The time:** 17 minutes and 53.9 seconds

But, as they say in the disclaimer: "Do not try this yourself at home."

---

# Rolled Salmon and Egg Sandwich

*Ellen Talbot*

Ogden, Utah

3 hard-boiled eggs, finely chopped
1 7½-ounce can salmon, drained, skin removed, and
    mashed
2 tablespoons mayonnaise
1 teaspoon mustard
½ teaspoon lemon juice

½ teaspoon Worcestershire sauce
dash dill
dash salt
dash pepper
4 slices soft white bread

Combine eggs, salmon, mayonnaise, mustard, lemon juice, Worcestershire sauce, dill, salt, and pepper. Set aside.

Overlap 2 slices of bread and roll out to flatten. Do the same with the remaining two slices.

Divide the salmon and egg filling into two portions. Spread onto flattened bread. Gently roll up the flattened bread slices with filling. Hold roll-ups in place with toothpicks.

*Yield: 2 roll-up sandwiches*

## CHEERFUL ANTICIPATION BEFORE . . . GOOD MEMORIES AFTER

Vacation travel is a very important and enjoyable time, not just the days actually spent away from home, but also the anticipation and planning before, and the memories and recharged feeling after the trip. A pleasant and interesting addition to put in a packed lunch would be brochures of the places that are soon to be visited and then, after returning to work, photographs taken and other souvenirs to keep alive the good memories.

Stephanie Hirsch<br>
West Palm Beach, Florida

# BAGEL AND LOX
## *Patty Frey*
### NEW BERLIN, WISCONSIN

2 ounces cream cheese, softened
1 bagel, sliced
¼ pound sliced smoked salmon

lettuce
4 thin tomato slices
2 thin onion slices

Spread cream cheese onto bagel and then layer salmon, lettuce, tomato, and onion.
Yield: 1 sandwich

Think of Dagwood Bumstead gleefully grabbing whatever he can find in the refrigerator and piling it layer upon layer upon layer between slices of bread to make a tower of chicken, cheese, lettuce, tomato, vegetables, ketchup, mustard, mayonnaise, and other eatables. He has been enjoying his culinary creation in a cartoon strip for more than 50 years, in 28 *Blondie* movies between 1938 and 1950, and in two television series that were shown in 1954 and 1968.

The exact birthdate of the "Dagwood Sandwich" was April 16, 1936, when cartoonist Murat B. Young had Dagwood make his first signature sandwich in the comic strip.

It may not be the easiest thing to wrap up and take for lunch, since you would need a suitcase in place of a lunchbox, but who can resist the appeal of a real "Dagwood Sandwich"?

# DATE-NUT SANDWICH
*Melanie Gill*
## ROCHESTER, NEW YORK

2 ounces cream cheese
2 slices date-nut bread

½ apple, peeled, cored, and thinly sliced
½ cup shredded Colby cheese

Spread cream cheese on date-nut bread. Place apple slices and Colby cheese on top of cream cheese.
*Yield: 1 sandwich*

---

## DON'T LEAVE HOME WITHOUT IT

Airline meals are not always the best because of the quality of the food and the way it is served in the little plastic trays (except, of course, if you are flying first class—but few of us do). As an alternative to eating the lunches served on airplanes, bring your own. The idea is not to have just a homemade sandwich or salad but also the little things that make it special. Include a nice plate and cup (of china or decorated paper), real silverware, and a cloth napkin. You will be the envy of those seated around you. Also include a large self-sealing plastic sandwich bag to put the reusable things in when you are finished, since it is not practical to start washing dishes and silverware at 35,000 feet.

Norman Weiss
Towson, Maryland

# Peanut Butter (Etc.) Sandwich

*Greer Olson*

Midland, Texas

½ cup peanut butter
2 slices oat bread
1 tablespoon honey mustard

¼ cup shredded cheddar cheese
1 medium apple, cored and thinly sliced

Spread peanut butter on one slice of oat bread and honey mustard on the other slice of bread. Sprinkle cheese over peanut butter and cover with apple slices and bread slice with honey mustard.

*Yield: 1 sandwich*

# NEXT-DAY HAMBURGER SANDWICH
## Julia Frazier
### GRANDVIEW, MISSOURI

1 tablespoon ketchup mixed with 1 tablespoon
  mayonnaise
1 hamburger roll, sliced in half
1 leftover hamburger

2 slices Muenster cheese
1 small onion slice
3 mushrooms, sliced
3 sweet pickles, sliced in half lengthwise

Spread ketchup-and-mayonnaise mixture on both halves of the hamburger roll.
Stack, in order, hamburger, Muenster cheese, onion, mushrooms, and pickles.
Yield: 1 sandwich

---

## SHAPE UP YOUR LUNCHES

There is no reason why sandwiches always have to be in the shape of the bread as it comes out of the package. Use different kinds of cookie cutters to cut the bread slices so you will have sandwiches shaped like hearts, stars, and holiday designs. Use the cut-off portions as croutons or bread crumbs.

Diane Mason
Indianapolis, Indiana

# Nutty Tuna Fruit in a Pita Pocket

*Natalie McDonald*

Euclid, Ohio

1 6⅛-ounce can tuna, drained
½ cup finely chopped apples
¼ cup finely chopped grapes

¼ cup finely chopped walnuts or pecans
mayonnaise
1 pita pocket

Combine tuna, apples, grapes, and walnuts, plus just enough mayonnaise to hold it together. Spoon into pita pocket.
*Yield: 1 sandwich*

---

## Lunchtime for Your Ears Too

If you eat lunch alone but you are in a situation where you cannot readily read a book, why not have one of those small portable tape players with earphones and listen to books on tape while you eat?

Greta Wright
Des Moines, Iowa

# SAUTÉED VEGGIES ON ITALIAN ROLLS

*Cicely Neff*

BEECH GROVE, INDIANA

3 medium zucchini, thinly sliced
1 small eggplant, thinly sliced
1 red pepper, thinly sliced
1 to 2 tablespoons olive oil

dash salt
dash pepper
2 Italian torpedo rolls
1 tablespoon sesame seeds

Sauté zucchini, eggplant, and pepper in olive oil in a large pan until well done. Sprinkle with salt and pepper. Slice torpedo rolls and fill with sautéed vegetables. Sprinkle with sesame seeds.
*Yield: 2 sandwiches*

---

## HUSH, HUSH. . . . MUM'S THE WORD. . . . IT'S A SECRET

Every few days, put a "Secret Bag" in your child's lunchbox. It can hold a special little toy, a picture, a small book, or something else that would be fun. The Secret Bag is completely wrapped up so the child cannot see what is inside and has absolute instructions with dire warnings about the "awful things that will happen to you if you open it before lunchtime."

Cynthia Ostrander
Schenectady, New York

# Cottage Cheese Confetti Pocket
*Florence Patton*
HADDONFIELD, NEW JERSEY

1 cup cottage cheese
½ cup finely chopped celery
¼ cup finely chopped carrots
6 pitted black olives, chopped

¼ cup chopped macadamia nuts
1 tablespoon chopped chives
1 pita pocket

Combine cottage cheese, celery, carrots, olives, macadamia nuts, and chives and spoon into pita pocket.
*Yield: 1 sandwich*

## The Benefits of Planning Ahead

There isn't always enough time or energy to cut up fresh cold vegetables each morning to put into a lunchbox. Many vegetables, such as carrots, celery, and broccoli, can be cut up in larger quantities in advance, then taken out in individual portions over the next several days, and packed with lunches. Be sure to store the cut-up vegetables properly in sealed containers in the refrigerator.

Linda Garcia
Amarillo, Texas

# Is This a Great Chicken Salad Sandwich or What?

*Emily Freeman*

## High Point, North Carolina

2 cups finely chopped cooked chicken
1 medium avocado, pitted, peeled, and mashed
1 tablespoon plain yogurt
½ tablespoon ketchup

dash celery salt
dash dill
4 slices oat bran bread
¼ cup alfalfa sprouts

Mix together chicken, avocado, yogurt, ketchup, celery salt, and dill.
Spread on bread and sprinkle with alfalfa sprouts.
*Yield: 2 sandwiches*

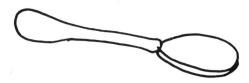

Brown bags were first made in the United States in Pennsylvania around 1850. About 20 years later, Francis Wolle received a patent for a machine that made the flat-bottomed, easy-to-fold bag that is used by just about everyone, everywhere, for just about everything, including packed lunches.

It took nearly 100 years—until the 1950s—for "brown bagging" to become the popular phrase for carrying your lunch to school or work.

Actually, "brown-bagging your lunch" sounds a whole lot more sensible than "Wolle-bagging your lunch," unless you are a descendant of Francis. But then again, you might still be receiving royalties on your great-great-grandfather's invention.

# Ham and Egg Sandwich
## *Gail Key*
### Bartlett, Tennessee

1 tablespoon mustard
2 tablespoons mayonnaise
dash hot sauce
4 slices white bread

4 thick slices ham
4 hard-boiled eggs, sliced
4 slices tomato
lettuce

Mix together mustard, mayonnaise, and hot sauce and spread on all four slices of bread. On two of the bread slices, layer ham, eggs, tomato, and lettuce. Cover with remaining two slices of bread.
*Yield: 2 sandwiches*

---

## Make the Lunchbox a Mailbox

Receiving mail is always a treat for young children, and what could be better to include in their lunchboxes than letters addressed to them personally, even if it is "fake" mail? Write a little note, seal it in an envelope, address the envelope to your child, and then draw your own funny little stamp in the upper right-hand corner. Their friends will always be asking, "What did you get in the mail today?"
Claudia Palmer
Bountiful, Utah

---

# COLBY WITH SUN-DRIED TOMATOES SANDWICH

*Norma Knutson*

TACOMA, WASHINGTON

mustard to taste
1 hard roll, sliced
1 tablespoon parsley
¼ teaspoon dill
lettuce

½ cup chopped sun-dried tomatoes soaked in
    1 teaspoon olive oil
3 slices Colby cheese
1 onion (Vidalia onion when in season), sliced

Spread mustard on hard roll. Sprinkle parsley and dill on mustard. Layer with lettuce, tomatoes, Colby cheese, and onion.
*Yield: 1 sandwich*

---

## FOOD FOR THE MIND AS WELL AS THE BODY

Include in the lunchbox—for either a child or an adult—an article about a well-known person, event, or current issue, and that evening have a discussion about what was covered in the article. This is a good way to get someone thinking about a particular subject.

Donna Fox
Holyoke, Massachusetts

---

The popularity of bagels has spread from New York City to the rest of the United States, and now close to one billion of those hard, round rolls are baked and eaten in the country each year.

Once it was just a plain bun to be eaten with cream cheese and, if you were blessed, lox. Now, however, there are so many varieties that it surely "bagels" the mind. You can get the traditional plain, egg, sesame, onion, and poppy seed bagels, of course, but the newest creations include cinnamon-raisin, jalapeño pepper, sun-dried tomato, oat bran, swirl, and spinach bagels.

And on St. Patrick's Day, you can get green bagels.

# Stuffed Salmon Sandwich
## *Trudy Gibson*
### Newport News, Virginia

1 7½-ounce can salmon, drained, skin removed, and
    mashed; or 1 6⅛-ounce can tuna, drained and
    mashed
4 slices bacon, well cooked and crumbled

3 tablespoons plain yogurt
2 teaspoons chili sauce
2 pita pockets

Combine salmon, bacon, yogurt, and chili sauce.
Spoon into pita pockets.
*Yield: 2 sandwiches*

---

### One Picture Makes a Thousand Smiles

Children always like to see themselves in photographs. They will get a particular charge out of finding in their lunchboxes Polaroid pictures of themselves that were taken that very morning or the night before.

Erika Crawford
Sacramento, California

# Good Stuff Sandwich

*Gail Barrett*

St. Paul, Minnesota

½ cup creamy peanut butter
2 slices whole wheat bread
¼ cup granola

1 avocado, pitted, peeled, and sliced
¼ cup alfalfa sprouts

Spread peanut butter on both slices of bread and sprinkle with granola. Spread avocado slices on one bread slice and sprinkle alfalfa sprouts over top. Cover with other slice of bread.

*Yield: 1 sandwich*

In a contest conducted by *New York* magazine in the summer of 1994 asking for the name of a make-believe new television program and its plot, one of the winning entries was "Make My Lunch"—Clint Eastwood hosts a gourmet cooking show in which great chefs of the world are forced to prepare their specialties at gunpoint.

# Jammin' Chicken Sandwich
## *Philip Lawson*
### Columbia Heights, Minnesota

1 cup chopped cooked chicken
¼ cup chopped pecans
2 tablespoons apricot jam

2 tablespoons sunflower seeds
1 hard roll, sliced

Combine chicken, pecans, jam, and sunflower seeds and spread on roll.
*Yield: 1 sandwich*

---

### Lunchtime Laughs

Nothing is funnier and more enjoyable than a good cartoon. Get several good cartoon books, cut out one or two selections a day, and put them in the lunchbox you are preparing. And, of course, don't let the person whose lunch you are making read the cartoon book in advance.

Lloyd Hayes
San Mateo, California

# Mushroom Roll-Ups

*Emily Harwood*

EUGENE, OREGON

2 cups chopped mushrooms
¼ cup Madeira wine
1 tablespoon mustard

4 ounces cream cheese, softened
4 slices soft multigrain bread

Sauté well mushrooms with Madeira wine.

Remove mushrooms from heat, drain, and let cool. Add mustard and cream cheese, mixing thoroughly. Set aside.

Overlap two slices of bread, and roll out until flat. Repeat with other two slices.

Divide mushrooms and cream cheese into two portions and spread onto flattened bread. Carefully roll up bread slices and secure with toothpicks.

*Yield: 2 roll-up sandwiches*

---

## IT DOESN'T ALWAYS HAVE TO LOOK LIKE LUNCH

Get a book that shows how to make fancy hors d'oeuvres from pieces of vegetables, fruit, cheeses, meats, and other foods, and include several of these items in each lunch. They will give a festive and happy look to the lunch as it is taken out of the lunchbox.

Diane Goodwin
Shawnee, Kansas

# TURKEY CHEESE POCKET
*Flora Wilkens*
GERMANTOWN, TENNESSEE

1 cup chopped turkey
¼ cup crumbled Gorgonzola cheese or blue cheese
2 tablespoons mayonnaise

1 teaspoon ketchup
1 tablespoon dill
1 pita pocket

Combine turkey, Gorgonzola cheese, mayonnaise, ketchup, and dill. Spoon into pita pocket.
*Yield: 1 sandwich*

# CREAM CHEESE AND OLIVES SANDWICH
## *Michael Gross*
### AURORA, COLORADO

2 ounces cream cheese, softened
1 soft roll, sliced
1 teaspoon dill

lettuce
1 small cucumber, peeled and sliced
8 green olives with pimientos, sliced

Spread cream cheese on both slices of roll. Sprinkle dill on cream cheese. Layer lettuce, cucumber, and olives on cream cheese on bottom half of roll.
*Yield: 1 sandwich*

Some of the best places to eat your lunch surely must be:

- Sandwich, Illinois
- Mayo, Florida
- Rye, Colorado
- Hambone, California
- Bread Loaf, Vermont

- Cheddar, South Carolina
- Cook, Nebraska
- Apple Valley, Minnesota
- Orange, New Jersey
- Fruitland, Tennessee
- Buttermilk, Kansas
- Coffee, Georgia
- Soda, Texas

# HEARTY AND HEALTHY SANDWICH
## *Mary Sutton*
### TULSA, OKLAHOMA

8 dates, finely chopped
5 large figs or prunes, finely chopped
¼ cup finely chopped pecans

2 tablespoons currants
1 tablespoon grated orange rind
2 slices whole wheat bread

Mix together dates, figs, pecans, currants, and orange rind. Form into a patty and place on bread.
*Yield: 1 sandwich*

---

The word *lunch* comes from the Spanish word *lonja*, meaning "slice," and originally referred to a slice or piece of food eaten during the day.

Until the early part of the 19th century, the midday meal was called "dinner" and the evening meal was "supper." "Lunch," a shortened form of "luncheon," began to be used in everyday language about 175 years ago.

# HEARTY TUNA SANDWICH
## Angela Moss
### CHICAGO, ILLINOIS

1 12½-ounce can tuna, drained
3 tablespoons mayonnaise
½ cup finely chopped walnuts

¼ teaspoon dill
½ cup grated cheddar cheese
4 slices rye bread

Mix together tuna, mayonnaise, walnuts, dill, and cheddar cheese and spread on bread.
Yield: 2 sandwiches

## MAKE EVERY DAY—WELL, ALMOST EVERY DAY—A HOLIDAY

It can be really enjoyable to pack theme lunches with appropriate food, wrappings, decorations, and novelties for different holidays, events, and seasons.

You can even make up your own holidays or special events and build lunches around them.
Meredith Dodson
Homewood, Alabama

# Minced Clam Sandwich

*Arlene Kirkland*

PASADENA, TEXAS

1 6½-ounce can minced clams, drained
3 ounces cream cheese, softened
2 tablespoons finely chopped onion

1 teaspoon Worcestershire sauce
¼ teaspoon dry mustard
2 slices rye or pumpernickel bread

Combine minced clams, cream cheese, onion, Worcestershire sauce, and mustard.
Spread on bread.
*Yield: 1 sandwich*

According to the NPD Group, Inc., of Park Ridge, Illinois, a company that conducts market research on eating trends throughout the United States, the five most popular sandwiches that children take to school are, in order:

1. peanut butter and jelly (of course)
2. ham
3. bologna
4. cheese
5. turkey

# TURKEY DINNER SANDWICH
## *Pauline O'Brien*
### LAKE WORTH, FLORIDA

$\frac{1}{2}$ *cup whole berry cranberry sauce*
*1 cup leftover stuffing*
*lettuce*

*2 hard rolls*
*4 large slices leftover turkey*
*1 tablespoon mayonnaise*

Mix together cranberry sauce and stuffing. Set aside.

Place lettuce on bottom half of rolls. Spread stuffing and cranberry sauce mixture onto lettuce. Cover with turkey slices. Set aside.

Spread mayonnaise on top halves of rolls and cover turkey.

*Yield: 2 sandwiches*

# LEFTOVER POTATO SALAD—PLUS SANDWICH
*Bonnie Sylvester*
NEW BRITAIN, CONNECTICUT

1 cup well-mashed potato salad
1 cup small pieces cooked ham

$\frac{1}{2}$ cup shredded cheddar cheese
1 dill pickle, chopped
4 slices bread

Combine potato salad, ham, cheddar cheese, and pickle, and spread on bread.
*Yield: 2 sandwiches.*

---

## IT'S EASIER WHEN YOU SHARE THE WORK

Making lunch every day for work can be a hassle. Try this with four of your coworkers. Assign each person a day in the workweek. Each one makes five lunches on his or her assigned day, thereby supplying all five of you with lunches. Although making five lunches is no small task, it is much more efficient and easier to make five at one time for one day, than one every day for five days. Of course, your group must first determine any particular likes and dislikes, food allergies, or religious restrictions of the people whose lunches you are making.

Esther Dionne
East Providence, Rhode Island

# 6

## Entrées to Go

*With main dishes that taste great and travel well,*
*you'll feel as though you're eating at home.*

(All of the entrées in this chapter are delicious when served cold, but
they can be heated up just before eating if you prefer.)

# Vegetable Lasagna

*Rita French*

BEAVERTON, OREGON

10 ounces chopped broccoli, cooked and drained
10 ounces chopped spinach, cooked and drained
⅓ cup finely chopped onion
1 clove garlic, minced
1 tablespoon basil
1 tablespoon parsley
1 teaspoon oregano
½ cup wheat germ
3 8-ounce cans tomato sauce

1 6-ounce can tomato paste
1 teaspoon olive oil
dash salt
dash pepper
9 lasagna noodles, cooked and drained
1 pound ricotta cheese
8 ounces mozzarella cheese, grated
½ cup grated Parmesan cheese

Preheat oven to 350°F.

Mix together broccoli, spinach, onion, garlic, basil, parsley, oregano, wheat germ, 2 cans of the tomato sauce, tomato paste, olive oil, salt, and pepper. Set aside.

Place 3 lasagna noodles on the bottom of a greased 9- by 13-inch pan. Spread half of the vegetable mixture evenly over top of the noodles. In turn, spread half of the ricotta cheese, sprinkle half of the mozzarella cheese, and then half of the Parmesan cheese over top. Make another layer of 3 lasagna noodles. Add the remaining vegetable mixture. Then spread the remaining half of the ricotta cheese and sprinkle the mozzarella cheese and then the Parmesan cheese, minus 1 tablespoon, over top.

Cover with the remaining 3 lasagna noodles. Pour remaining can of tomato sauce over noodles. Sprinkle with remaining 1 tablespoon Parmesan cheese.

Bake for 40 to 50 minutes at 350°F.

Remove from oven and let cool.

Cut into 3- by 4-inch pieces.

*Yield: 9 servings*

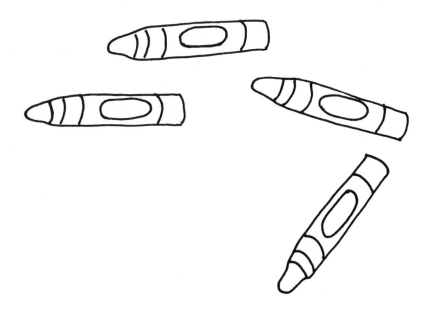

Every November the maker of Ziploc sandwich bags sponsors the "Ziploc National Sandwich Day," a sandwich recipe contest for elementary-school children in grades 1 through 6.

The winning sandwiches are selected on the basis of creativity and nutrition from recipes sent in by schoolchildren throughout the country. The winning entries are included in a cookbook published by DowBrands, the maker of Ziploc bags.

Some of the winners and finalists:

- The "United Nations Sandwich," by New York 5th grader Aislynn Poquette, includes Italian bread, French dressing, Swiss cheese, German sauerkraut, Irish corned beef, American cheese, and Russian dressing.
- The "Texas Sandwich," by Texas 4th grader Jennifer Cohen, combines barbecued beef, cheddar cheese, and jalapeño peppers.
- The "Creamy Raisin Delight Sandwich," by California 1st grader Mikkael Lewis, contains cream cheese, raisins, grated carrots, and chopped ham.
- The "Steak-o-Rama Sandwich," by Arkansas 5th grader Trent McDaniel, calls for chopped steak, provolone cheese, bacon, Worcestershire sauce, pineapple, and an olive.
- The "Apples-and-Stuff Sandwich," by Rhode Island 1st grader Rebecca Neveux, mixes apple butter, wheat germ, honey, raisins, and apples.

For more information about the Ziploc National Sandwich Day Contest and how to enter, write to:

Ziploc National Sandwich Day
DowBrands Food Care Division
P.O. Box 68511
Indianapolis, IN 46268

# FRANKS FOR THE BEANS

*Carol Bryant*

SLIDELL, LOUISIANA

4 hot dogs, thinly sliced
½ cup chopped onion
½ cup ketchup
½ cup brown sugar

1 teaspoon mustard
2 tablespoons barbecue sauce
1 16-ounce can pork and beans
1 16-ounce can garbanzo beans

Fry hot dogs and onions in a large, heavy pan until lightly browned. Set aside.

Mix together ketchup, brown sugar, mustard, barbecue sauce, pork and beans, and garbanzo beans. Pour into pan with hot dogs and onions.

Simmer for about 20 minutes, stirring frequently.

*Yield: 4 servings*

# Baked Salmon Loaf

*Jenny Feldman*

## Newton, Massachusetts

1 7½-ounce can salmon, drained, with bones and skin removed
¾ cup bread crumbs
2 tablespoons margarine or butter, melted

1 10½-ounce can tomato soup
2 eggs, beaten
2 tablespoons grated onion
2 tablespoons grated Parmesan cheese

Preheat oven to 350°F.
Mash salmon and add bread crumbs, margarine, tomato soup, eggs, and onion.
Spoon into a greased loaf pan, patting down with slightly dampened hands. Sprinkle with Parmesan cheese.
Bake for 50 minutes at 350°F.
*Yield: 6 servings*

## Prior Planning Prevents Panic Packing

You don't have to be a military strategist to do menu planning for a week or even a month in advance. There are many advantages to planning ahead. You can see what you have on hand and what you have to buy at the store; you can arrange for variety; you can plan jointly with the people whose lunches you pack; you can take into account special events and arrangements; and, best of all, you avoid those night-before and early morning panics of "What can I make for lunch?"

Cathy Britton
Lowell, Massachusetts

# Noodle Pudding
## Miriam Lewandowski
### Newark, Delaware

8 ounces thin noodles, cooked and drained
1 cup sugar
8 ounces cream cheese, softened
1 cup margarine, softened

8 eggs, beaten
2 teaspoons vanilla
2 tablespoons grated Romano and Parmesan cheese

Preheat oven to 350°F.
Mix together noodles, sugar, cream cheese, margarine, eggs, and vanilla.
Pour noodle mixture into a greased 3-quart baking dish.
Sprinkle Romano and Parmesan cheese over top.
Bake for 1 hour and 15 minutes at 350°F.
Remove from oven and let cool completely.
Cut into squares.
*Yield: 6 to 8 servings*

---

### Yes . . . Elegance in a Lunchbox

In addition to the food packed for the lunch, include a cloth or colorful napkin, a placemat, real silverware, a nice glass for a beverage, and a designer paper plate or even a china plate. In other words, there is much more to lunch than just the food you put in your mouth.

Claire Butler
Omaha, Nebraska

# COLD CHEESE AND BROCCOLI PIE
## *Iris Knight*
### MIDWEST CITY, OKLAHOMA

6 ounces cheddar cheese, broken into small pieces
12 ounces ricotta cheese
12 ounces cottage cheese
1 pound finely chopped broccoli, cooked and well
    drained

2 eggs
3 ounces cream cheese
1 teaspoon dill
dash mint
1 8½-ounce package corn muffin mix

Preheat oven to 350°F.

Mix together cheddar cheese, ricotta cheese, cottage cheese, cooked broccoli, eggs, cream cheese, dill, and mint.

Spoon into a greased 9- by 13-inch pan. Set aside.

Prepare corn muffin mix according to package directions. Spread evenly over top of uncooked pie in pan. Bake for 40 to 45 minutes at 350°F.

Remove from oven and let cool. Cut into approximately 3-inch squares.

*Yield: 12 servings*

# Tasty Meat Loaf
*Ina Stanley*
## Dunbar, West Virginia

1½ pounds ground beef
2 eggs
2 tablespoons barbecue sauce

1 cup shredded mozzarella cheese
½ cup chopped celery
3 tablespoons ketchup

Preheat oven to 350°F.

Mix together ground beef, eggs, barbecue sauce, ¾ cup of the mozzarella cheese, and celery. Pat into shape and put into a 2-quart baking dish. Cover with ketchup and sprinkle with remaining ¼ cup mozzarella cheese.

Bake for approximately 1 hour at 350°F.

Remove from oven, let cool, and cut into slices.

*Yield: 6 servings*

## Two Good Ideas

Since peer pressure can be so strong among children in all grades, and it is a rare child who wants to appear different from everyone else, here are two suggestions to follow when packing lunch: (1) Check with other parents or the teacher to see what is the "in" lunch (and lunchbox) for kids if yours is starting at a new school. (2) If you plan to put something really different in your child's lunchbox, ask other parents to include the same thing so your child will not be the only one with something new.

Karen Cohen
West Allis, Wisconsin

# Very Nice Rice

*Cara Quintana*

SANTA FE, NEW MEXICO

¼ cup margarine
¾ cup confectioners' sugar
grated peel of 1 lemon
3 eggs

½ cup white raisins
½ cup chopped walnuts
3 cups cooked rice
1 cup cooked peas

Preheat oven to 350°F.
Cream margarine and sugar. Add lemon peel and eggs, one at a time. Stir in raisins, walnuts, rice, and peas.
Spoon into a greased 1½-quart baking pan.
Bake for 50 to 60 minutes at 350°F.
*Yield: 8 to 10 servings*

---

## IT'S NOT ONLY WHAT YOU CARRY, BUT THE WAY YOU CARRY IT

There are a lot more ways for children to carry their lunch to school than just in a lunchbox or in a plain paper bag. There are reusable insulated bags, backpacks, and small, hard-sided, insulated totes, to name just a few. Do not surprise your child by going out and choosing a lunch carrier without having him or her help pick it out. Carrying the "right" lunch container that is acceptable to the peer group is important, and, as you can imagine, carrying the "wrong" one could be a disaster.

Teresa Johnson
Laurel, Maryland

# Lunchtime Lasagna

*Mindy Trombley*

Troy, New York

1 pound ground beef, cooked and well drained
½ cup chopped onion
2 celery stalks, scraped and cut into small pieces
1 green pepper, chopped into small pieces
2 6-ounce cans tomato paste
1½ cups water
¼ teaspoon thyme
1 teaspoon Worcestershire sauce

dash salt
dash pepper
1 1-pound package lasagna noodles, cooked and
    drained
2 pounds ricotta cheese
12 ounces mozzarella cheese, grated
¼ cup grated Parmesan cheese

Preheat oven to 350°F.

Mix together cooked ground beef, onion, celery, green pepper, tomato paste, water, thyme, Worcestershire sauce, salt, and pepper. Set aside.

Line the bottom of a greased 9- by 13-inch pan with a single layer of cooked lasagna noodles. Spread half of beef mixture over top of lasagna noodles. Spread half of the ricotta cheese and then half of the mozzarella cheese over top. Place another single layer of lasagna noodles on top. Spread remaning half of beef mixture over top, and then spread remaining half of the ricotta cheese, followed by the remaining half of the mozzarella. Cover with a single layer of lasagna noodles. Sprinkle Parmesan cheese over top.

Bake for 40 to 50 minutes at 350°F.

Remove from oven and let cool.

Cut into 3- by 4-inch pieces.

*Yield: 9 servings*

## MAY I TAKE YOUR ORDER, PLEASE?

Include in the lunchbox each day a handwritten menu with an ordering form—or, if you have a home computer, a fancy computer-generated order form—offering what is available for the next day's lunch. It could be a fun thing to do, choosing and filling out a menu order form, and the person getting the food will be assured of having what he or she likes for lunch. Make sure you have available or can easily get the choices that are offered. This menu idea can be used for schoolchildren of all ages, as well as for adults who take their lunch to work.

Holly Page
Scottsdale, Arizona

# FRUIT AND NUT PASTA SQUARES
## *Lynne Parker*
### GASTONIA, NORTH CAROLINA

¼ cup margarine, softened
½ cup light brown sugar
2 eggs
¼ cup sugar
¼ teaspoon salt
½ teaspoon cinnamon

1 tablespoon lemon juice
2 teaspoons grated lemon rind
8 ounces egg noodles, cooked and drained
½ cup pitted and chopped dried fruit
½ cup raisins
½ cup chopped nuts

Preheat oven to 350°F.

Spread margarine on the bottom and sides of an 8-inch square pan. Sprinkle brown sugar over margarine. Set aside.

In a large bowl, mix together eggs, sugar, salt, cinnamon, lemon juice, lemon rind, cooked egg noodles, dried fruit, raisins, and nuts.

Spoon mixture evenly into pan.

Bake for 40 to 50 minutes at 350°F until pasta is set and golden brown.

Remove from oven, let cool completely, and then invert onto plate.

Cut into 2- by 4-inch squares.

*Yield: 8 servings*

Napoleon III, emperor of France from 1852 to 1870 and nephew of Napoleon Bonaparte, could be called the "Godfather of Margarine."

In the 1860s he sponsored a contest in France to find an inexpensive substitute for butter. The winner was a chemist named Hippolyte Mège-Mouries.

The word *margarine* comes from the Greek word *margaron*, meaning "pearl," because of margarine's original pearly color.

# 7

## Salads, Crudités, and Dips

*Your lunchbox will sparkle with fresh greens and vegetables
for healthy choices and great new tastes.*

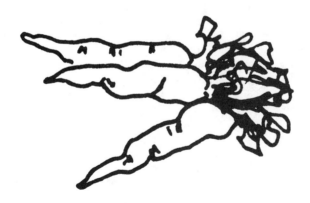

# ABSOLUTELY ATHENIAN
*Marcia Farnsworth*
HUDSON, NEW HAMPSHIRE

½ small head lettuce
1 large tomato, cut into wedges
1 small onion, cut into rings
1 green pepper, chopped
1 cucumber, peeled and sliced
4 green olives, sliced in half
4 black olives, sliced in half

2 hard-boiled eggs, cut into wedges
4 ounces feta cheese, crumbled
3 anchovies, cut into small pieces
olive oil
vinegar
pita bread

Chop lettuce into small pieces and place in a food storage bag or container. Set aside.

Combine tomato, onion, green pepper, cucumber, green olives, black olives, eggs, feta cheese, and anchovies. Mix in oil and vinegar to taste. Place in a separate food storage bag or container.

Just before serving, mix together lettuce and rest of salad.

Serve with pita bread.

*Yield: 2 servings*

Considering the popularity of lettuce and how much is eaten in salads and in so many sandwiches, it is surprising to learn that it has taken such a long time for lettuce to be accepted and widely grown as a commercial crop.

Christopher Columbus brought this vegetable with him to America, but for 400 years it was grown only in small amounts in home gardens. It was not until the early 1900s that demand for it increased, and then it became profitable to grow large volumes of lettuce commercially.

One could say that lettuce was just "a-head" of its time.

# GUACAMOLE DIP
## Roberta Grimes
### PLEASANT HILL, IOWA

2 large avocados, pitted, peeled, and mashed
1/4 cup lemon juice
1 garlic clove, crushed
1/2 cup finely chopped onion

1/2 cup sour cream
tortilla chips
carrot sticks, celery sticks, broccoli, cauliflower,
    cucumber sticks, and zucchini sticks

Combine avocados, lemon juice, garlic, onion, and sour cream, mixing together until smooth. Pack in serving-size containers and chill.

When preparing your lunchbox, pack tortilla chips and vegetables in separate baggies or containers. Use the guacamole as a dip for these finger foods at lunchtime.

*Yield: 2 servings*

Saran Wrap was invented in 1941 for use as a wrapping film for weapons and other equipment, to protect them against weather, rust, and other harmful elements. It was later discovered that the protection this plastic film offered equipment could also shield foods from the harmful effects of odors and air.

What started as military research for World War II led to the introduction of Saran Wrap into the consumer marketplace in 1953.

# Hawaiian Cottage Salad

*Barbara Donahue*

Honolulu, Hawaii

½ cup crushed and drained pineapple
2 kiwis, peeled, sliced, and cut into pieces
3 tablespoons flaked coconut

¼ cup chopped macadamia nuts
2 cups cottage cheese
¼ cup dried cranberries

Mix together pineapple, kiwis, coconut, macadamia nuts, cottage cheese, and cranberries.
*Yield: 2 servings*

The Roaring Twenties in the United States saw the creation of numerous salad dressings that were varying combinations of mayonnaise, pimientos, chili sauce, green peppers, chives, onions, horseradish, and sometimes even caviar. Because of that last ingredient, or because the mixtures looked like what was served on salads in Russia, the sauces became known collectively as "Russian dressing," although their origins had no true connections with that country.

Today, the Russian dressing that is frequently served is a mere combination of mayonnaise and ketchup, devoid of the more interesting and costly ingredients.

It is sad to say, and perhaps reminiscent of the breakup of the Soviet Union, which resulted in a far less significant Russia, that time has diminished the élan of American-made Russian dressing.

# CHICKEN-CORN SALAD

*Grace Kuhn*

HARRISBURG, PENNSYLVANIA

2 cups chopped cooked chicken
2 cups cooked corn
½ cup finely chopped green pepper
½ cup finely chopped red pepper

¼ cup chopped pimientos
1 tablespoon relish
2 to 3 tablespoons mayonnaise

Mix together chicken, corn, green pepper, red pepper, pimientos, relish, and mayonnaise.
*Yield: 2 servings*

To most children, that combination of shredded cabbage, shredded carrots, mayonnaise, and maybe raisins, is "cold slaw," and, indeed, it is usually served cold. But the origin of the name has nothing to do with temperature.

"Coleslaw" comes from the Dutch word *koolsla*, a joining of *kool* ("cabbage") and *sla* ("salad"); therefore, cabbage salad.

But no matter what you call it, it sure perks up a sandwich and makes a tangy side dish.

# Bow-Tie Salad Special

*Bevery Vaccaro*

## White Plains, New York

2 cups bow-tie pasta, cooked and cooled
$\frac{3}{4}$ cup fresh chopped broccoli
$\frac{3}{4}$ cup chopped carrots
$\frac{1}{2}$ cup chopped red or green pepper
$1\frac{1}{2}$ cups grated cheddar cheese
$\frac{1}{2}$ cup chopped walnuts

$\frac{1}{2}$ cup chopped sweet pickles
$\frac{1}{4}$ cup sweet pickle juice
5 tablespoons plain yogurt
5 tablespoons mayonnaise
salt
pepper

Mix together bow-tie pasta, broccoli, carrots, red pepper, cheddar cheese, walnuts, pickles, pickle juice, yogurt, mayonnaise, salt, and pepper.

*Yield: 4 to 6 servings*

Depending on which story you believe, that popular white spread used on countless sandwiches each day should be called either "bayonnaise" or "mayonnaise," both with French connections dating back to the 1700s when it was first created. One claim is that a chef in Bayonne, France, created the stuff and, therefore, it should be named in honor of his city.

But a story with perhaps more historical accuracy, or at least a better promotional angle, is that the chef of the duke of Richelieu was making a special dinner to celebrate the French victory in 1756 over the British at Port Mahon, the capital city of the Mediterranean island of Minorca. His menu called for a sauce made from cream and eggs, but there was no cream. The duke's chef substituted cooking oil for the absent cream, mixed together the oil, eggs, and seasonings, and thereby created "Mahonnaise."

Actually, the origin of the word *mayonnaise* is even more obscure—and full of contradictions. Some people believe that it came from the French word *manier*, meaning "to stir," while others say *mayonnaise* had its origins in the old French word *moyeu*, meaning "egg yolk."

However it got its name, mayonnaise in the United States follows the style of the recipe created and served by Richard Hellmann and his wife at their delicatessen on Columbus Avenue in New York City in 1903. CPC International acquired Hellmann's mayonnaise, and it is now sold under that name east of the Rocky Mountains and under the brand name Best Foods west of the Rockies. Together these brands account for nearly half of all the mayonnaise sold in the United States.

There is a myth that mayonnaise causes food poisoning. The truth is that the acidity of the vinegar and lemon juice in commercially produced mayonnaise acts to retard the growth of bacteria. The problem of spoilage comes not from the mayonnaise, but from the food that is mixed with it, such as eggs, potato, tuna, and chicken. Those foods have a greater tendency to go bad when subject to warm weather than does mayonnaise.

Homemade mayonnaise can be hazardous when it is made with raw eggs. Moreover, it does not contain preservatives that allow for a longer shelf life. The bacteria in eggs used in commercially prepared mayonnaise are killed by pasteurization.

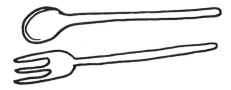

# Limeapple Salad
*Hope Rowe*
## Frankfort, Kentucky

1 3-ounce package lime gelatin dissolved in $\frac{3}{4}$ cup
   boiling water
$\frac{3}{4}$ cup crushed canned pineapple in its own juice

1 cup lowfat or nonfat cottage cheese
1 cup lowfat sour cream

Stir into dissolved gelatin the pineapple, cottage cheese, and sour cream.
Chill overnight.
*Yield: 3 servings*

---

### Napkins Are Not Just for Wiping Your Hands

Rather than just putting plain napkins in a lunchbox, use them as blank pages to draw pictures, write notes, or convey wishes. Each note or picture should have a connection with a holiday or with something your child likes or is doing at the time.

Michelle Hagen
Everett, Washington

# Potato and Ham Together Salad
## *Pia Chandler*
### Seattle, Washington

1 cup cooked potato cubes
1 cup cooked ham cubes
¼ cup chopped celery
5 black olives, chopped
3 tablespoons chopped pimientos

1 tablespoon minced onion
1 small garlic clove, crushed
1 teaspoon brown mustard
⅓ cup mayonnaise

Mix together potato cubes, ham cubes, celery, black olives, pimientos, onion, garlic, mustard, and mayonnaise.

*Yield: 2 servings*

---

### A Nice Way to Say "It's Mine, Hands Off"

If you work in a place where a lot of people bring their lunches in brown paper bags and there is a chance lunches could get mixed up in the office refrigerator, supply yourself with preprinted, decorated bags. That way, yours won't be taken by mistake and you have a more subtle and dignified safeguard than can be achieved by writing your name in big letters on the outside of the bag.

Carina Quellette
Highland Park, Michigan

# Tuna-Artichoke Salad

*Grace Norwood*

KNOXVILLE, TENNESSEE

1 12½-ounce can tuna fish, drained and crumbled
1 14-ounce can artichoke hearts, drained and chopped
¼ cup chopped celery

¼ cup chopped carrots
1 to 2 tablespoons mayonnaise
1 teaspoon mustard

Lightly toss together tuna fish, artichoke hearts, celery, carrots, mayonnaise, and mustard.
*Yield: 2 servings*

## READ THE FINE PRINT

In the last few years more and more "snack-sized" or "portion-sized" foods have become available in the stores. Although they might be convenient and even cute to include in a packed lunch, carefully check out the extra cost you are paying for that convenience, what the ingredients are, and the listed nutritional information. You can't always tell what you are eating just by the slick and appealing name on the label. You might find it much less expensive—and much more healthful—to create your own individual-sized snacks using ingredients that you buy in bulk and then "repackage" in Ziploc bags.

Andrew Morgan
Columbia, South Carolina

# COLD SPINACH SALAD
## *Jill Wooten*
### MAPLEWOOD, NEW JERSEY

6 spinach leaves, chopped
1 large carrot, grated
1 celery stalk, chopped
10 green olives stuffed with pimientos, chopped

10 black olives, chopped
2 tablespoons chopped fresh dill
4 radishes, thinly sliced
French dressing to taste

Mix together spinach, carrot, celery, green olives, black olives, dill, and radishes.
Mix in French dressing.
*Yield: 2 servings*

---

### CONVENIENT, INEXPENSIVE, REUSABLE, AND REPLACEABLE

Although plastic sandwich bags and plastic and foil wraps are convenient, another way to pack lunch is in reusable plastic containers. It is best to use the least expensive containers you can buy, since some of them most certainly will be lost during the school year and will have to be replaced.

Lucy Dupree
Decatur, Georgia

# SHRIMP DIP DELIGHT
## *Dale Hickey*
### PROVIDENCE, RHODE ISLAND

1 10½-ounce can tomato soup
8 ounces cream cheese
2 teaspoons unflavored gelatin, dissolved in ½ cup cold
    water
1 cup mayonnaise

8 ounces cooked shrimp, mashed
½ cup finely chopped onion
½ cup finely chopped green pepper
½ cup finely chopped celery
crackers or hearty bread

Cook tomato soup and cream cheese in a heavy saucepan over low heat until cream cheese melts. Mix well. Stir in dissolved gelatin.

Remove from heat and let cool about 15 minutes.

Mix in mayonnaise, shrimp, onion, green pepper, and celery.

Pour into a bowl and chill for several hours.

Spread on crackers or hearty bread.

*Yield: 4 to 6 servings*

---

Those baked rolls covered on top with onion flakes are called bialies (singular: bialy) because they are named after Bialystok, Poland, where they are traditionally baked and eaten with great enthusiasm.

# CHICKEN RICE SALAD

*Jennifer Ramsey*

BONNER SPRINGS, KANSAS

1 cup cooked rice, chilled
1 cup diced cooked chicken, chilled
3 tablespoons chopped scallion
1 carrot, grated

6 green olives with pimientos, chopped
2 tablespoons Dijon mustard
1 tablespoon parsley
$\frac{1}{4}$ teaspoon dill

Mix together rice, chicken, scallion, carrot, olives, mustard, parsley, and dill.
*Yield: 2 servings*

---

There is no reason that anyone has to take a whole sandwich of any one kind, especially if you are making lunch for two or more people. For example, you can make one ham and cheese sandwich and one peanut butter and jelly sandwich, and then put half of each sandwich in each lunchbox. That way, both people have a variety for lunch.

Sheryl Michaud
West Hartford, Connecticut

# TOMATO AND MOZZARELLA MERGER
### *Martin Gautreaux*
#### METAIRIE, LOUISIANA

3 large tomatoes, chopped
¼ cup olive oil
1 garlic clove, crushed
2 teaspoons lemon juice
salt

pepper
¾ cup grated mozzarella cheese
4 spinach leaves, cut into pieces
Italian bread

Mix together tomatoes, olive oil, garlic, lemon juice, salt, and pepper. Set aside and let sit in refrigerator overnight.

Combine mozzarella cheese, spinach, and tomato mixture just before serving.

Serve with Italian bread.

*Yield: 2 servings*

There are many packaged seasoning salts available in food stores, but it is easy and inexpensive to make your own custom blends at home.

Using a mortar and pestle makes it convenient to crush and blend salt with various spices and herbs, but you can do the same job with a sturdy dish and a heavy spoon.

Choose the spices and herbs that appeal to you and experiment with different combinations. Make small amounts at first until you find the mixture you like, and then produce a good supply. Keep an accurate list of the ingredients you use, and the exact amounts of each one, so you can make more later.

Store in a closed container.

# SUPER HAM AND CHEESE SALAD
## *Terry Myers*
### CHARLESTON, WEST VIRGINIA

1 cup cooked ham cubes
1 cup Swiss cheese cubes
$\frac{1}{4}$ cup chopped sweet pickles
2 apples, cored and chopped

$\frac{1}{4}$ cup raisins
$\frac{1}{4}$ cup coarsely chopped pecans
2 tablespoons mayonnaise or plain yogurt

Mix together ham cubes, Swiss cheese cubes, pickles, apples, raisins, pecans, and mayonnaise.
*Yield: 2 servings*

---

### PACKING FOR ROMANCE

Have an office romance in mind? Think about a "lunchbox date," where you pack lunch for two and include special foods, real silverware, china plates, placemats, and other niceties for the two of you to spread out on your desks, the conference-room table, or outside in a nearby park.

Gary Lambert
North Las Vegas, Nevada

# 8

## BEVERAGES

*These drinks will slake your thirst with great taste and complement your lunch with real panache.*

# Brandied Iced Coffee

*Lori Norton*

OXNARD, CALIFORNIA

1 cup cooled coffee
½ ounce brandy
1 tablespoon heavy cream

dash cinnamon
dash nutmeg
sugar to taste

Mix together coffee and brandy. Stir in heavy cream, cinnamon, nutmeg, and sugar. Chill thoroughly.
*Yield: 1 serving*

Those ubiquitous little drink boxes filled with milk, juice, and other beverages have become extremely popular since the early 1980s. Now, close to three billion of them are emptied by thirsty sippers each year.

# MINTY REFRESHER

*Ann Curtis*

## CORONADO, CALIFORNIA

juice of ½ orange
juice of ½ grapefruit
1 quart prepared iced tea

½ orange, sliced
1 sprig fresh mint

Stir orange juice and grapefruit juice into iced tea. Add orange slice and mint.
Stir well just before serving.
*Yield: 2 servings*

# Think Neat for Outdoor Eating

Nothing is more pleasant than eating your lunch outside on a nice day, rather than sitting inside with your usual lunch spread out all over your desk. Therefore, consider packing a more compact, less messy, easy-to-eat lunch for those sunny days when you don't want to eat indoors. Some examples of less-messy lunches follow:

- egg salad in a plastic container eaten with a fork along with some crackers, rather than an egg salad sandwich
- sandwiches made with sliced cold cuts rather than with tuna, egg, or shrimp salad
- sandwiches made with less mustard or ketchup than usual, and without the kinds of garnishes that will fall out easily
- one-dish entrées that can be eaten right out of a plastic travel container with a fork or spoon
- dry crackers and pretzels rather than potato chips
- juice in a single-serving pack with its own straw, rather than a drink that must be poured into a cup from a container
- fruit cut into small pieces and eaten with a toothpick instead of whole fruits that may be too juicy or messy to eat while sitting on a park bench or cross-legged on the ground
- hard cookies and other finger-food desserts instead of crumbly layer cake

Lucille Williams
Rockville, Maryland

# ORANGE CRANBERRY PUNCH
## *Margaret Kraus*
### TEMPE, ARIZONA

1½ cups cold orange juice
1½ cups cold cranberry juice cocktail

1 teaspoon lemon juice
1 cup cold seltzer

Mix together orange juice, cranberry juice, and lemon juice. Stir in seltzer. Pour into a container and seal tightly.

*Yield: 2 servings*

---

### GOOD THINGS COME IN FEDERAL EXPRESS AND UPS PACKAGES

If a group of you brings your lunch and eats it together in a company dining room, think of ordering a special gourmet cake or dessert from a mail-order company to celebrate someone's birthday, anniversary, or promotion. Most mail-order food companies offer overnight delivery, so you can specify exactly when you want the food to arrive. And don't forget to tell everyone the day before to leave out dessert when they pack lunch for the next day.

Briana Davis
Burton, Michigan

# ICED GINGER TEA
*Sharon Powell*
MONTGOMERY, ALABAMA

*juice of ½ medium lemon*
*1 teaspoon ground ginger*

*1 quart prepared iced tea*
*2 orange slices, cut into quarters*

Stir lemon juice and ginger into iced tea. Add quartered orange slices.
Let sit overnight in refrigerator.
*Yield: 2 servings*

Marvin Chester Stone, who lived in Washington, D.C., at the turn of the century, is rarely mentioned in any history books, but he was a truly innovative man whose idea affects our everyday life.

Until 1890, if you wanted to sip a drink you had to use a stalk of rye or some other type of natural hollow stem. Then there was a great improvement. Mr. Stone created a drinking straw made from manila paper coated with wax. And, of course, he received a patent for his new invention. Since that humble beginning, drinking straws have evolved to today's "bendy" plastic straws, with flexible, accordionlike sections that offer comfort, convenience, and ease of motion for greater enjoyment of your favorite beverages.

Some people might say that Marvin Chester Stone's invention is one of the few really useful things to come out of Washington in the last 100 years.

# 9

# Desserts and Fruits

*These treats will make great finales for your lunchbox meals.*

# APRICOT PECAN BREAD
*Kimberly Maxwell*
## MARIETTA, GEORGIA

1¼ cups flour
2 teaspoons baking powder
¼ teaspoon salt
¼ teaspoon baking soda
½ cup light brown sugar, firmly packed
½ cup chopped dried apricots

½ cup chopped pecans
1 teaspoon grated orange peel
1 egg
¾ cup milk
¼ cup oil

Preheat oven to 350°F.

Mix together flour, baking powder, salt, and baking soda. Add in brown sugar, apricots, pecans, orange peel, egg, milk, and oil. Mix together well.

Scrape batter into a greased loaf pan.

Bake for 45 to 50 minutes at 350°F, until toothpick tests clean.

*Yield: 1 loaf*

## Heavy Trading in the Lunchbox Market

Trading of lunchbox contents is common in school, so include one or more tradeable items in your child's lunchbox. The things to be traded should not be elaborate; keep them as simple and as inexpensive as possible. Some very marketable trading items include the following: packaged cakes; homemade cookies; little, inexpensive toys or games; a section of a sandwich that has been cut into quarters; a baseball, a football, or other kind of trading card; a small book; a souvenir trinket from a tourist attraction; and colored pencils. The list is limited only by your imagination, your source of supplies, and the particular characteristics of the local lunchtime trading market where your children go to school.

Joyce Ellis
Biloxi, Mississippi

# BOYSENBERRY COFFEE CAKE
*Denise Dudley*
## CHESAPEAKE, VIRGINIA

$\frac{1}{4}$ cup butter or margarine, softened
1 cup sugar
2 eggs
1 teaspoon raspberry brandy
1 cup sour cream
2 cups flour

1 teaspoon baking powder
dash salt
1 15-ounce can boysenberries, drained
1 cup brown sugar
1$\frac{1}{2}$ teaspoons cinnamon
$\frac{1}{2}$ cup chopped walnuts

Preheat oven to 350°F.

Cream butter and sugar. Mix in eggs, brandy, and sour cream. Stir in flour, baking powder, and salt.

Pour half of the batter into a greased and floured 8-inch-square pan. Cover with drained boysenberries. Sprinkle $\frac{1}{2}$ cup of the brown sugar, 1 teaspoon cinnamon, and $\frac{1}{4}$ cup walnuts over top. Cover with remaining half of the batter. Sprinkle remaining $\frac{1}{2}$ cup brown sugar, $\frac{1}{2}$ teaspoon cinnamon, and $\frac{1}{4}$ cup walnuts over batter.

Run knife through batter to marbleize.

Bake for about 1 hour, until toothpick tests clean, at 350°F.

Remove from oven and let cool.

Cut into approximately 3-inch squares.

*Yield: 9 servings*

## Eat Healthy, Eat Neat

Fruit is a great thing to bring for lunch, but it can sometimes be messy and troublesome to eat at your desk, especially if you work with a computer. You can avoid this problem if you peel (if necessary) and then cut up the fruit into bite-sized pieces and eat them with a toothpick or small fork.

Elizabeth Hartman
Alexandria, Virginia

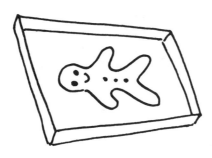

# Cinnamon Ginger Snap Cookies

*Phyllis Morse*

### Bellevue, Washington

$\frac{3}{4}$ cup margarine, softened
1 cup sugar
1 egg
$\frac{1}{4}$ cup molasses
2 cups flour

1 tablespoon ginger
2 teaspoons baking soda
1 teaspoon cinnamon
dash salt
1 teaspoon cinnamon mixed with $\frac{1}{4}$ cup sugar

Preheat oven to 350°F.

Beat margarine and sugar until light and fluffy. Add in egg and molasses, beating well. Stir in flour, ginger, baking soda, cinnamon, and salt.

Roll batter into 1-inch balls and coat with cinnamon-and-sugar mixture.

Place cookie balls on greased cookie sheet 2 inches apart.

Bake for 10 to 12 minutes, until lightly browned, at 350°F.

Remove cookies from cookie sheet and cool on wire rack.

*Yield: 6 dozen cookies*

## Anytime Can Be Lunchtime

Since some people get hungry before lunchtime rolls around, pack a mini-lunch snack, such as crackers with jelly, a piece of fruit, a cookie, or something that is easily eaten and will not take away from the main lunch. This "pre-lunch" should be wrapped and marked separately from the main lunch. The same idea can be used for an afternoon "post-lunch," as a treat later in the day.

Francis Ross
Anchorage, Alaska

# DATE 'N' NUT NIBBLES

*Kim Eaton*

## INDEPENDENCE, MISSOURI

2 eggs
1 cup sugar
1 cup flour
1½ teaspoons baking powder

dash salt
1 teaspoon orange extract
2 cups chopped dates
1 cup chopped pecans

Preheat oven to 325°F.

Beat eggs and sugar until very light. Slowly mix in flour, baking powder, salt, orange extract, dates, and pecans.

Spoon mixture into a greased and floured 8-inch square pan. Pat down with dampened hands.

Bake for 25 to 30 minutes at 325°F.

Remove from oven and let cool.

Cut into 2-inch squares.

*Yield: 16 squares*

## IT'S NOT WHAT YOU SAY BUT THE WAY YOU SAY IT

Finding a list of errands to do on the way home from work is not the most pleasant lunchbox surprise. However, an errand list can be sugarcoated by adding some extra special treats in the lunchbox with notes inside detailing the errands to be done. For example, it is much more agreeable to find a wrapped extra-rich cookie with a note saying, "This is for picking up the dry cleaning," or an attached Post-it note declaring, "Your favorite muffin here is the reward for filling the gas tank at the service station on the way home."

Patsy Blum
Hamilton, Ohio

# FRUITY TOPSY-TURVY CAKE

*Beth Covington*

LIVONIA, MICHIGAN

$\frac{1}{2}$ cup margarine, softened
2 cups brown sugar
2 peaches, pitted and thinly sliced
2 pears, cored and thinly sliced
3 tablespoons margarine
6 tablespoons milk

3 eggs, beaten until light
1 cup sugar
1 cup flour
1 teaspoon baking powder
1 teaspoon vanilla

Preheat oven to 350°F.

Spread $\frac{1}{2}$ cup softened margarine in an 8-inch square pan. Sprinkle brown sugar over margarine in pan. Arrange peach slices and pear slices evenly over brown sugar. Set aside.

Combine 3 tablespoons margarine with milk and cook over low heat until margarine melts. Stir well and remove from heat. Set aside.

Mix together eggs, sugar, flour, baking powder, and vanilla. Stir in margarine-and-milk mixture. Spoon batter over fruit slices.

Bake for 50 to 60 minutes, until toothpick tests clean, at 350°F.

Remove from oven and let cool.

Invert cake onto plate and cut into approximately 2 $\frac{1}{2}$-inch squares.

*Yield: 9 squares*

# The Next Best Thing to Winning the Lottery

As a surprise for special days, include in the packed lunch a handmade coupon saying that it is redeemable for a present at a particular store where the person eating the lunch has wanted something. Call ahead or stop by to make the arrangements with the store so the surprise gift can be readily picked up by the recipient. This idea works well for both children and adults.

Etta Grabowski
Waukesha, Wisconsin

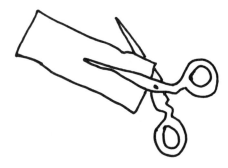

# Chocolate Peanut Butter Bites

*Jeanette Pena*

CLEARWATER, FLORIDA

½ cup margarine
1 cup graham cracker crumbs
½ cup flaked coconut

½ cup chunky peanut butter
½ cup chocolate chips
1 14-ounce can sweetened condensed milk

Preheat oven to 375°F.

Melt margarine and pour into a 9- by 13-inch pan, covering bottom evenly.

Sprinkle graham cracker crumbs and then coconut evenly over margarine in pan. Set aside.

Melt peanut butter and pour into pan, evenly covering graham cracker crumbs and coconut. Sprinkle chocolate chips over top and then cover evenly with milk.

Bake for 25 minutes at 375°F.

Remove from oven and let cool.

Cut into 2-inch squares.

*Yield: 2 dozen squares*

Although yogurt was first brought to the United States in the 1780s by Turkish immigrants, it did not become popular here until after the end of World War II.

At about that time Daniel Carasso arrived in this country from Spain and started making Dannon (named after himself, Daniel) yogurt in New York City. His clever innovation that encouraged many people to try this product was the addition of strawberry fruit preserves to create the first "sundae-style" yogurt.

In addition, sales were greatly helped by an excerpt from Benjamin Gaylord Hauser's book *Look Younger, Live Longer* that appeared in the *Reader's Digest* in October 1950, and by the growing interest in health foods during the 1960s.

About one billion containers of yogurt a year are sold today in the United States. Strawberry is the most popular flavor.

# Quick Peach Cobbler

*Allison Perkins*

## Winchester, Kentucky

4 large fresh peaches, pitted, halved, and cut into slices
1 tablespoon brown sugar
¼ teaspoon cinnamon

2 teaspoons margarine or butter
2 tablespoons orange juice
10 ladyfingers, cut into pieces

Combine peaches, brown sugar, cinnamon, margarine, and orange juice in a heavy saucepan, and cook over very low heat for about 15 minutes until mixture is thick and bubbly.

Remove from heat and gently stir in ladyfinger pieces.

*Yield: 2 servings*

---

### As They Say, "Some Like It Hot"

A nice change from the usual cold lunches would be hot foods. If your office or workplace does not have a microwave oven, persuade the company to put one in or organize a campaign and get your coworkers to chip in and buy a microwave. Then all can greatly expand their lunchbox options by bringing food that can be heated up.

Jessica Coyle
Cherry Hill, New Jersey

# Desk Trail Bars
*Jackie Moulton*
SOUTH PORTLAND, MAINE

1½ *pounds melted chocolate—milk, dark,*
   *or a combination*
½ *cup honey*
¼ *cup currants*
½ *cup chopped dried pears*
¼ *cup chopped dried figs*

¼ *cup chopped pitted dates*
½ *cup flaked coconut*
1 *cup chopped nuts*
½ *cup wheat germ*
¾ *cup quick oats*

Combine melted chocolate, honey, currants, pears, figs, dates, coconut, nuts, wheat germ, and oats, mixing together thoroughly.

Spoon mixture into a greased 9- by 13-inch pan. Pat down with dampened hands.

Cut into 2-inch squares.

*Yield: 2 dozen squares*

---

## LET THE BIDDING BEGIN . . . FOR A WORTHY CAUSE

Many charitable groups have fund-raising events at which products and services from local businesses, professionals, and residents are auctioned off. Your contribution to the list of items auctioned-off could be a week of homemade lunches delivered to the workplace of the lucky bidder. Your donation makes lunchtime a "good works" time.

Anita Giordano
New Rochelle, New York

# ORANGE ALMOND POUND CAKE

## Leslie Bishop

### NAPERVILLE, ILLINOIS

1¼ cups sugar
½ cup butter
2 eggs, beaten
1½ teaspoons almond extract
grated rind of 1 orange

1½ cups flour
½ cup milk
1½ teaspoons baking powder
¼ teaspoon salt
juice of 1 orange

Preheat oven to 350°F.

Cream 1 cup of the sugar with butter. Add eggs, almond extract, orange rind, flour, milk, baking powder, and salt, mixing together well.

Pour batter into a greased loaf pan.

Bake for 55 to 60 minutes at 350°F.

Remove from oven and set aside.

Mix together remaining ¼ cup of sugar and orange juice and pour over cake.

Cut into 1½-inch slices.

*Yield: 6 servings*

Hardly anyone knows it, but the Twinkle Toe Shoes Company of St. Louis plays an important part in a million and a half treats eaten every day in the United States.

Back in 1930 during the Great Depression, James A. Dewar, manager of the Continental Bakery in Chicago, wanted to increase sales by creating a new, inexpensive snack cake. Continental already made and sold "Little Short Cake Fingers," but that was only during the six weeks of the strawberry season. Mr. Dewar noticed that the aluminum pans used to make those cakes just sat idle the rest of the year.

Taking advantage of that underachieving resource, he created a little cake with something inside that could be sold all year round. And what could be a better name for them than "Twinkies"?

Except for the filling, Twinkies have changed very little since they were first introduced. The original banana-flavored creme inside was changed to vanilla-flavored creme in the 1940s.

Twinkies were created for children, but they have become a favorite of snack-eaters of all ages. Indeed, Twinkies were a regular item in Archie Bunker's lunchbox; they have been served at a dinner at the White House; and they had center stage as the birthday cake at Superman's 50th birthday party.

And the St. Louis connection?

While Mr. Dewar was developing his new snack cake, he saw a billboard in St. Louis advertising Twinkle Toe Shoes and thought it would be the perfect name—with a minor alteration—for his new cakes.

# BRANDIED FRUIT MEDLEY

*Tracy Ferraro*

GREENWICH, CONNECTICUT

*1 pound dried fruit, cut into small pieces*
*1 lemon, sliced and seeded*
*1 cinnamon stick*

*water*
*¼ cup apricot brandy*

Preheat oven to 350°F.

Combine dried fruit, lemon slices, and cinnamon stick in a 1½-quart baking dish. Add enough water to cover half of the fruit.

Bake for 1 hour, until fruit is tender and water has been absorbed.

Remove from oven and mix in apricot brandy.

Chill in refrigerator.

*Yield: 4 to 6 servings*

---

### NO MORE FORGETTING YOUR LUNCH

Sometimes it can be hectic in the morning getting ready for work, and you rush out of the house forgetting your lunch. Here is a suggestion if you drive to work. As soon as you pack your lunch, put your car keys in with the lunch. Now you cannot leave home without taking your lunch along with you.

Wendy Hess
Parma, Ohio

# Sesame Seed Peanut Butter Squares

*Christy Carpenter*

GAINESVILLE, FLORIDA

½ cup chunky peanut butter
½ cup honey
1 cup powdered milk

¼ cup flaked coconut
1 cup sesame seeds

Heat peanut butter and honey in a heavy saucepan over low heat, stirring frequently, until peanut butter melts and blends with the honey.

Remove from heat and mix in powdered milk, coconut, and sesame seeds.

Spoon mixture into a greased 8-inch square pan, patting down with slightly dampened hands.

Let cool and cut into 2-inch squares.

*Yield: 16 squares*

---

### FLOWER POWER

Nothing perks up a dining room table like fresh flowers, and the same enjoyment can be transferred, on a smaller scale, to lunchtime. Include in your packed lunch a freshly cut flower or two, gently wrapped first in a wet paper towel and then in aluminum foil, along with a small vase. Set up the flowers at your desk, or wherever you eat your lunch, to give your surroundings a small touch of elegance.

Katherine Christensen
Lincoln, Nebraska

# HONEY-ALMOND SQUARES
## *Lillian King*
### WASHINGTON, D.C.

6 tablespoons honey
1¼ cups confectioners' sugar
1 cup sliced almonds
1 cup flour
2 tablespoons flaked coconut

2 tablespoons orange juice
½ tablespoon grated orange peel
dash nutmeg
dash cloves

Combine honey and sugar in a heavy saucepan and bring to a boil over medium heat. Add almonds, stirring well.

Remove from heat and stir in flour, coconut, orange juice, orange peel, nutmeg, and cloves.

Stir mixture well, transfer to a greased bowl, cover, and chill in refrigerator overnight.

Preheat oven to 375°F.

Using a greased rolling pin on a greased surface, roll out dough to approximately ½-inch thick. Place dough into a greased 8-inch square pan.

Bake for 25 to 30 minutes at 375°F.

Remove from oven and let cool.

Cut into 2-inch squares.

*Yield: 16 squares*

# Fresh Fruit Cocktail

*Maxine Rooney*

## Takoma Park, Maryland

sections from 1 large grapefruit
1 apple, cored and cut into chunks
sections from 1 large orange
$\frac{1}{2}$ cup grapes, cut into halves

$\frac{1}{4}$ cup raisins or currants
$\frac{1}{4}$ cup coarsely chopped pecans
2 tablespoons orange juice
2 tablespoons ginger ale

Combine in a large bowl the grapefruit, apple, orange, grapes, raisins, pecans, orange juice, and ginger ale. Chill.
*Yield: 2 servings*

---

## It's the Right Thing to Do

Recycling is becoming more and more widespread and is even required by law in many places. When you include soda or juice bottles or cans in your lunch, be sure not to dump them into the waste can with your other trash. Separate and place them in recycling containers. If necessary, take the empty drink containers home with you for recycling with your other household bottles and cans.

Brad Heindel
State College, Pennsylvania

# INDEX